# MAKE YOUR OWN
# LUCK

# MAKE YOUR OWN
# LUCK

## 12 Practical Steps to Taking
## Smarter Risks in Business

### EILEEN C. SHAPIRO and
### HOWARD H. STEVENSON

PORTFOLIO
Published by the Penguin Group
Penguin Group (USA) Inc., 375 Hudson Street, New York, New York 10014, U.S.A.
Penguin Group (Canada), 10 Alcorn Avenue, Toronto, Ontario, Canada M4V 3B2
(a division of Pearson Penguin Canada Inc.)
Penguin Books Ltd, 80 Strand, London WC2R 0RL, England
Penguin Ireland, 25 St. Stephen's Green, Dublin 2, Ireland
(a division of Penguin Books Ltd)
Penguin Books Australia Ltd, 250 Camberwell Road, Camberwell, Victoria 3124,
Australia (a division of Pearson Australia Group Pty Ltd)
Penguin Books India Pvt Ltd, 11 Community Centre, Panchsheel Park,
New Delhi – 110 017, India
Penguin Group (NZ), Cnr Airborne and Rosedale Roads, Albany, Auckland 1310,
New Zealand (a division of Pearson New Zealand Ltd)
Penguin Books (South Africa) (Pty) Ltd, 24 Sturdee Avenue, Rosebank,
Johannesburg 2196, South Africa

Penguin Books Ltd, Registered Offices: 80 Strand, London WC2R 0RL, England

First published in 2005 by Portfolio, a member of Penguin Group (USA) Inc.

1  3  5  7  9  10  8  6  4  2

Publisher's Note: This publication is designed to provide accurate and authoritative information in regard to the subject matter covered. It is sold with the understanding that the publisher is not engaged in rendering legal, accounting, or other professional services. If you require legal advice or other expert assistance, you should seek the services of a competent professional.

LIBRARY OF CONGRESS CATALOGING-IN-PUBLICATION DATA

Shapiro, Eileen C.
    Make your own luck : 12 practical steps to taking smarter risks in business / Eileen C.
Shapiro, Howard H. Stevenson.
        p. cm.
    Includes bibliographical reference and index.
    ISBN 1-59184-077-5
    1. Strategic planning. 2. Risk. 3. Decision making. 4. Industrial management. I. Stevenson, Howard H. II. Title.
HD30.28.S4182 2005
658.4'012—dc22      2004065490

Printed in the United States of America
*Designed by Joy O'Meara*

*To Ben and Fredericka,*
*the best bets we've made*
*in our lives*

*In uncertainty*
*lies*
*opportunity.*

— Albert Einstein


*Only if*
*you bet smart.*

— Eileen Shapiro and
Howard Stevenson

# Contents

# Welcome

## to the World of Bets

# An Invitation

**THIS** is a book about bets—business bets, career bets, life bets—and how to up the odds that *your* bets will get you where you want to go. It's a book about bets because to get the results you desire, you don't want to depend on dumb luck. *You want to make your own luck and take greater control of your destiny.*

That's what Bill Gates and Warren Buffett and Oprah Winfrey have done. And that's what this book will help you to do.

We've gotten to the principles in this book through trial and error on our own investments and business bets, academic research, and our work with established enterprises and start-up companies around the world.

What we've learned is that upping the odds takes what we call "Predictive Intelligence" (PI)—the ability to act in the face of uncertainty to bring about desired results. And we've learned that anyone's PI, yours or ours, can be improved, just like any other set of skills.

First you have to recognize when you're in a betting situation.

Then you can follow twelve quick steps, which we call "The Gambler's Dozen," to increase your Predictive Intelligence and up the odds on your business and life bets.

If you're browsing through this book right now to see whether our approach will be helpful to you, we invite you to take the quick quiz on page 5—and then look at the answer key on page 6.

Eileen C. Shapiro
Howard H. Stevenson

P.S. Though we know that both of our seventh-grade English teachers—not to mention our editors at Portfolio—may be tearing their hair out, we have worked hard to write this book in a conversational style. So, where there are errors in grammar (including a "who" where a "whom" would be correct), you can be sure that the fault is ours.

# The Test

How often do you bet—
on behalf of your company and/or for yourself?

\_\_\_ a) Many times per day

\_\_\_ b) Once or twice per day

\_\_\_ c) Several times per week

\_\_\_ d) Several times per month

\_\_\_ e) Several times per quarter

\_\_\_ f) Several times per year

\_\_\_ g) Virtually never; I make it a policy not to gamble.

Please review the above list, and check the answer that is closest to your own experience. Then look at the answer key on the next page.

# THE ANSWER KEY . . . AND THE RATIONALE

**If you checked a, b, or c,** you've already mastered the first principle of Predictive Intelligence, which is *recognizing that every action is a bet.* All of us are always in betting situations—and always living with the consequences of the bets we've placed. This book is a bet too—you will lay out some money and spend some time, in hopes of a future return on this investment. Given that you already have the right mind-set, we think the odds are excellent that this book will pay off for you repeatedly.

**If you checked d, e, or f,** you probably recognize only your biggest or your most uncertain actions as bets—a decision about whether to get divorced, for example, or whether to commit to a new product line or technology for your company. You can use this book to help you up the odds on these big bets. As you do, we hope you'll also see that the same principles and steps will be helpful for the ongoing stream of other, smaller bets you face all the time.

**If you checked g,** you're in for a surprise, because this book will give you a radically new way of looking at your business and your life.

\*   \*   \*   \*

This book, and all our work, is based on the premise that every purposive action is a bet; one acts now on the expectation or hope, but not the certainty, of the results that will be achieved in the future. Or, as Alan Greenspan, chairman of the U.S. Federal Reserve, put it, "Human actions are always rooted in a forecast of those actions."

Humans are gambling animals. We all gamble, all the time. Every time we act, we invest time, or reputation, or effort, or money with no guarantee that the results that we seek, no matter how likely they may seem, will occur as we have planned—or as we will desire when the results occur. Once we've placed any of our assets at risk, we've placed a bet. Our bets may be large, a marriage or corporate merger; or small, a decision about where to have dinner or what the dress code will be for

an upcoming business meeting; but if they involve committing resources now to achieve some result in the future, our actions are bets.

No matter what our preferences, none of us can avoid gambling as
we live our lives. What we can do is use our Predictive Intelligence to
up the odds that, over time, the portfolio of bets we place will lead to
the kind of futures we envision or desire. Then we can go from depending on dumb luck to making our own luck and taking more control over our destinies.

And with that, we invite you to consider the General's Dilemma.

# The General's Dilemma

IMAGINE for a moment you are a general. It's war time, and you have just massed your troops for the next fight. This battle, you know, will be pivotal. The enemy has already gained the upper hand in virtually every aspect of the conflict and is continuing his drive into your territory. Worse still, the world's reigning superpower, which until this point has remained neutral, is about to throw its weight to the other side; through diplomatic channels you know that if you lose this battle, the balance of world opinion and power will shift to your adversary. What happens over the next several days will determine all.

Now an amazing thing happens. Two of your foot soldiers happen upon the enemy's masterplan for the upcoming battle, handwritten and mired in the mud, and make it their business to get the plan to you. This plan has everything: current locations of the adversary's troops, plans of attack, supply lines. A member of your staff instantly recognizes the handwriting as that of one of his (former) good friends, from before the war, and now an enemy and the assistant adjunct general to the top guy on the other side.

As you pore over the plans, you realize that the adversary's commander, a world-renowned strategist, has dangerously divided his forces. By brilliance or luck, your troops, who outnumber your adversary's by a factor of two to one, are closer to each of the pieces of your enemy's army than any of these pieces are to each other. This is the best bit of luck you can imagine. Immediately you see that if you move fast, you will destroy your adversary's forces and thereby end the war.

What do you do?

If you are a U.S. Civil War buff, you have already recognized this as the story of "the Lost Order" at the Battle of Antietam, fought along a creek in western Maryland. The generals in question were Robert E. Lee, the Confederate commander whose forces were dangerously divided, and George B. McClellan, general of the Army of the Potomac for the Union and the lucky recipient of the Lost Order.

In the actual case, McClellan did not act quickly. Instead he took the time to establish telegraph communications with the War Department in Washington; check with his superiors, including President Lincoln; consider his options; and make his usual final battlefield checks and preparations. Then he attacked, based on the enemy positions shown in the Lost Order. But the positions had changed. In the time that McClellan spent to decide on and execute his plan of action, parts of the Confederate army had reconnected and remassed, consolidating its positions and making it far less vulnerable to assault by McClellan's troops.

In the end, the Battle of Antietam was fought to a draw, despite the perfect information the North had received and despite the North's superior numbers (about 87,000 troops for the North versus about 40,000 for the South). It was a bloody day, the single bloodiest of the war, with over 20,000 casualties.

The U.S. Civil War could have been ended that week in September 1862. Instead, it dragged on for close to another three years, ultimately costing a total of 558,000 military deaths, more than the sum of all U.S. military deaths in all other wars including the Revolutionary War, both World Wars, and subsequent wars in Korea, Vietnam, and Iraq.

\* \* \* \*

McClellan had an abundance of assets. He worked for a powerful organization. He had the right title and, having graduated second in his class at West Point, the right credentials. At Antietam, he had superior troop strength and location and, through a stroke of luck, he was in possession of perfect information at the perfect time. But what he lacked on the battlefield may have been more important than all these assets combined: the Predictive Intelligence to act fast enough in the face of uncertainty to change his plans and grab the opportunity that good fortune had handed him.

Of course, acting in the face of uncertainty is scary, because you are acting before all the facts are in—though in truth you are always acting before all the facts are in, whether you are doing what you planned to do or making a shift based on new information. The higher your Predictive Intelligence, the more agile and fast you will be at making your own luck by identifying the best bets and then taking action when and while the opportunities are available.

People can have high PIs in some areas and stink in others—be great in love and poor in business; great at internal politics and poor in building lasting value; great in financial investments and poor in human relations; great at creating and inventing and poor in managing and growing. But in those areas in which individuals have high PIs, you can see it in their performance; they get more of what they want, more of the time, than other people

Bill Gates has a high PI in his areas of focus, and so do Warren Buffett, Oprah Winfrey, and Peter Lynch; Ronald Reagan and Robert E. Lee did too. Chili Palmer, the low-level Miami mobster who becomes a big-deal Hollywood movie producer in Elmore Leonard's novel *Get Shorty*, is a poster child for high PI. If you take a minute or two, you can probably list a dozen people from among those you know personally or have read about who seem to have better-than-average records in placing winning bets in some (but not necessarily all) areas of their lives.

This is more than *being* lucky; people with high PIs consistently make their own luck: they take whatever circumstances they are in and create bets with the best odds for getting them closer to the outcomes they seek. You can think of Predictive Intelligence as a kind of consistent street smarts applied to a series of goals, and especially to goals that will take a lot of steps and a lot of time to achieve.

And that's what this book is about: *how to increase the odds that your bets will get you or your organization to the future you desire by boosting your Predictive Intelligence.* That's making your own luck—and taking greater control of your destiny.

# You Bet Your Company (and Your Life)

**WHERE** you go to school, what your grades are, or how you do on standardized tests may help you get a better job, but none of these things necessarily indicates your level of Predictive Intelligence or helps you improve your PI (and in some cases precisely the reverse is true). But whatever your starting point, you can boost your PI and systematically up the odds on the bets you place on your own account or on behalf of your company.

Now, a question: if we asked you to diagram the key components that make up a bet, could you do it?

If you're willing, take a moment or two and sketch out your version here:

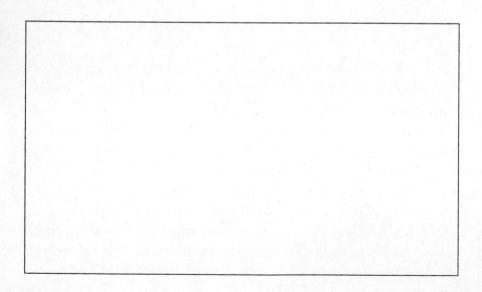

If you found this exercise tougher than you anticipated, we think you have plenty of company. In fact, we'd expect most people to struggle with this assignment. Even though all of us make life and company bets every day, few of us think consciously about the process we go through as we make our bets and live with the results.

You probably won't be surprised that we've thought a lot about how to diagram a bet so we can see the pieces and how they relate to each other. We've done this in the simplest way, by starting with the most obvious pieces and then adding the other components that, while equally important, are often not visible and therefore often not sufficiently taken into account.

The core of any bet is an action and a result; you fight a battle and then you win or lose. The simple flip-chart version looks like this:

## Action ➤ Result

This picture is correct as far as it goes, but it misses that every bet starts with an intent or desired result and ends with the level of satisfaction with the actual results achieved. Now we have this revised picture:

## *Intent* ➤ Action ➤ Result ➤ *Satisfaction*

We've put the two new pieces in italics because they are so often overlooked. While all of us act with intent, a lot of the time most of us are not consciously aware of what results we are working hardest to achieve. At Antietam, was McClellan putting his primary efforts into winning the battle—or into staying out of trouble with his bosses in Washington?

On the satisfaction side, many of us often assume that if we achieve the results we set out to achieve, we will be content. But of course that's not always true. Sometimes we end up with outcomes that are far different from what we had anticipated and even so find ourselves highly satisfied with the unexpected results. And other times we achieve exactly what we set out to achieve and then find ourselves a bit dissatisfied—or even more—as we experience these outcomes.

Now we come to the final piece. This one is fundamental to bets, Predictive Intelligence, and upping the odds, and it's ignored more often than any of the others.

Predictions.

Every bet is based on a set of predictions. You predict what you think you will want when your results are achieved, and those predictions shape the intents of your bets. You predict which actions will have what results and what other people will do in response, and those predictions shape the actions you choose to take.

Since we think predictions are the largely unseen foundation of all bets, we amend our diagram this way:

Now, here's the important thing about this picture. All human actions are based on intent, the desire to achieve results we think we will want when the results come to pass. But not all humans are equally good at predicting which actions will lead to what results, what factors could intervene, and what results we will value in the future. The difference, in our view, *is the level of Predictive Intelligence, how able each of us is to act in the face of uncertainty to bring about desired results.*

\* \* \* \*

As we've noted, it's a curious paradox. IQ tests and other standardized tests measure all sorts of things, but what they don't measure is *the ability to predict well.* So while those tests provide a good bit of information about a number of important skills, they aren't designed to measure, support, or build Predictive Intelligence and the ability to make your own luck.

Over time, and through our successes and our failures, we've come to understand that Predictive Intelligence is not an innate characteristic, something that some people are born with and others are not. Predictive Intelligence is a bundle of skills that can be improved, just like any other bundle of skills. We've parsed this bundle into a dozen skills, which we've dubbed the Gambler's Dozen, and which we've organized into a process we use as we craft and revise our own bets and as we work with other people to craft and revise theirs.

Each of these twelve skills provides a different way to look at the bets you're already engaged in or are about to place, from intent to satisfaction to predictions. Though there are some overlaps and fuzzy edges among these steps, we've found that sticking to the discipline of using them all gives the best results.

The rest of this book gives you our approach to building Predictive Intelligence and upping the odds using the Gambler's Dozen. We've ordered these steps in the sequence that seems to work best with groups and for us personally. We've given each step a "tag" and an overview question, which we explain in the chapters that follow.

The underlying organization of the Gambler's Dozen is an OOPA! process: *Orient, Organize, Predict*, and *Act!* (with an exclamation point after *Act!* because you can't create a great betting average if you figure out what to do . . . and then don't do it). The first six steps of this process focus primarily on the orienting and organizing part of OOPA—figuring out where you want to go and why, where you have been going, and where you need to make fast adjustments to your current plans. Steps 7 through 12 focus primarily on the predicting and acting parts—generating alternatives, getting a better fix on odds and outcomes of each, checking how well these bets will meet your purposes, and then selecting and placing the bets.

Here's an overview chart of the twelve steps, with their tags and summary questions:

# Build Your Predictive Intelligence
## The OOPA! Process

### Orient & Organize Steps

1. **The Big Goals:** What future am I trying to create?
2. **Upside/Downside:** Will this game be worth playing, for me?
3. **Jump Bets:** Do I need to make a radical shift now?
4. **Campaign Plans:** Who will I need and how will I get them?
5. **Implicit Strategy:** How much magic will my current bets require?
6. **Plan B:** What's the best I could do if my existing plan gets blocked?

### Predict & Act! Steps

7. **Prediction Maps:** What's the future space I'm betting into?
8. **Wallpaper Jujitsu:** What are my best "left side" bets?
9. **Risk Splits:** How much risk can I shed or shift?
10. **Point of Action:** What's the "it" I'm betting on?
11. **Domino Effects:** Will I be locked into a tight set of follow-on bets?
12. **Game Over:** How will I know when to call it quits?

Four things that we have discovered in our own experience, and that we urge you to consider as you modify the Gambler's Dozen for your own use, are these:

1. **Cover all the steps.** The Gambler's Dozen is second nature for some people, but everyone gets better at it when the process is made conscious and intentional. Covering all the steps also helps prevent errors of omission and other betting mistakes.

In fact, we find that many people have consistent patterns of betting mistakes; we do too. Eileen's tend to be in steps 3 and 4; Howard's in steps 4 and 6. Watching Martha Stewart, we'd guess her persistent errors are in steps 2 and 3. Whatever your pattern, we find the best way to up the odds is to go through all the steps. You may decide to cover them in a different order from the one we present here. Great. But cover them all.

2. **Write down your thinking for each step.** Rough sketches and notes are fine, but put your thoughts in writing. The reason for this is

simple: the act of writing forces crisper thinking. At Baupost, a private investment fund which Howard co-founded and now has $5 billion under management, the discipline of articulating all prospective bets in writing was ingrained as an early element of the culture and has been part of what has led to consistent 15 percent returns per year for the past twenty years. For our own bets, we've found even very rough notes consistently sharpen our assessments and spark better ideas.

3. **Go fast, especially for the first round.** And by fast, we mean real fast—literally seconds or minutes per question, rather than days or months. Then you can go back and refine, as necessary and as fits in the time window for the bets at hand. For small bets, such as how to respond to an important e-mail, you might take seconds per question. For large bets, such as strategy issues for a company, you might assemble a team and spend fifteen to thirty minutes per question, with a little bit more for certain steps (particularly steps 7 through 10), and dedicate a full day or two to the process.

We like going fast because we know that speed through the OOPA! process gives an edge in taking the most attractive initial positions and securing options on future positions. In war, the first guy who understands the terrain takes the high ground. In investing, the first guy who understands the territory gets the best prices. Those who take no action until the patterns are just about completely clear or until they have full and elegant assessments often find that the alternatives left to them, while more certain, are also disproportionately more expensive.

4. **Remember that the sole purpose of this process is to bet better.** If you begin to worry about getting an A+ in process management or about writing an analytic masterpiece that resolves all the uncertainties (and also takes longer than the window for attractive bets is open), please pause and remember the purpose of using the Gambler's Dozen is, once again, to bet better. And then get back to the business of actually creating and placing better bets—and achieving the future you wish to create.

\*    \*    \*    \*

We know, from our work with many executives, that at this point you still may not be convinced that the actions you take—from everyday ones about whether to stop for your daily latte or how much to study, to big ones about whom to marry or whether to buy this house or that one—are bets. And similarly, you may also see most of your actions at work, from how to handle a meeting to how to handle a product rollout, not so much as bets as "just the way we do business."

In either case, we again invite you to go through this book, consider the steps for boosting your PI and the accompanying examples, and try the process on a decision that you or your organization is facing. After you've reached the end, we think your views about the roles of bets in your personal life and your business life will have changed—and that you'll have begun to think differently about how to make your own luck and create the future you desire.

# Chapter Format

THE following twelve chapters all have the same format. Each starts with a teaser—a story with a twist, or a haiku or a limerick that we've created especially for the occasion. Then comes the body of the chapter, which describes the step and the skill on which it is based. We've included little quizzes and puzzles throughout, along with our answers and rationales.

We've also added an ending puzzle as the final part of each chapter. These puzzles are different from the other ones because we don't give you our answers to them. In fact, we've constructed these puzzles specifically not to have one "right" answer, only to have answers that are true for you or for your organization. You will find these puzzles more useful if you allow yourself to play around with them for a bit *and write down your answers before going to the next step.* (Try this—you'll see that it really does make a difference.)

We hope you have fun. And we hope that you find the Gambler's Dozen as useful as we have.

# OOPA!—
## Inside the Gambler's Dozen

# The
# Orient and Organize
# Steps

**The Gambler's Dozen, Step 1**

# THE BIG GOALS:
## Picture the Future You Want

## DOG HAIKU

Dog chases a bus.

Query: What will he do if

He catches the bus?

# 1. The Big Goals: What Future Am I Trying to Create?

YOU'RE stranded on a deserted island. If you could choose one person to be stranded with you, who would it be?

Before reading further, take a moment and jot down your answer here:

_____.

Over the years, we've heard all sorts of answers to the deserted-island question. Usually the person selected is one's spouse, a great philosopher or religious leader, a sexy movie star, or a famed teller of tales.

Then we heard Dean Kamen's response.

Dean Kamen is the inventor of the Segway personal transport system plus scores of other devices including a wheelchair that climbs stairs. When Kamen was asked the deserted-island question in the course of an interview, he thought for a moment and then said . . . the world's best boat builder.

Was this the first answer that occurred to you? Or something like it, such as the world's best survivalist?

Or, like both of us and most other people in our experience, was the first person you thought of someone you could live with on the island until you were rescued, or died?

\* \* \* \*

The first skill of Predictive Intelligence, and the one on which we base this step of the Gambler's Dozen, is identifying your Big Goals: imagining the future you want to create and envisioning what your life, or your company, will have to look like to achieve these goals. This is an OO—Orient and Organize—skill, and it is essential to smart betting whether you find yourself in a new situation, such as suddenly being stranded on an uninhabited island, or in a continuing situation, such as working on your company's strategy or figuring out how to manage your marriage.

Deciding on the big goals is critical because, in any situation, you have only a limited set of resources to place at risk—time, money, reputation, effort—what we call the "100 marbles." If you use up some or all of your 100 marbles on secondary or tertiary goals, like being entertained while stranded, you'll miss opportunities to achieve the results that you believe will bring you the most future satisfaction.

In some ways, getting clear on the big goals is even more important in ongoing situations than in new ones. In a new situation, you start with a clean slate, which prompts you to give at least cursory attention to your goals. In ongoing situations, you have legacy goals, objectives that you or others set some time ago. Then it becomes very tempting to keep doing what you've always been doing, under the implicit assumption that the original goals, or whatever the original goals have evolved into, still make sense.

That may have been the case for General Motors with its focus on beating Ford and the other U.S. automakers, and later for Mercedes with its focus on beating BMW and the other European automakers, when the real threat was Toyota and all its brands from Corolla to Lexus. (In the meantime, while GM and Mercedes were aiming to beat their traditional rivals, Toyota decided to aim at beating everyone and be the world's biggest automaker by 2010—and by 2003 had taken enough share from GM and Mercedes and all the others to have gained the number-two spot in terms of unit sales.)

The purpose of this step is to anchor your betting process in your view of the kind of future you want to create. It works the same for life bets and career bets as it does for business bets; to bet smart, start by creating a rough outline of the future you want to create for yourself or for your company. If, as one set of examples, you're in a marriage going bad, manage a long-term employee who is no longer performing satisfactorily, or find yourself in a job situation that you have begun to hate, you need to decide whether your goal is to get out or to make the best of a bad situation. Both kinds of goals are honorable, but they are different, and they will lead to very different kinds of bets as you go through the rest of the steps in the Gambler's Dozen.

We know from experience that even the mention of "futures" and "visions" or any combination of the words *objectives*, *goals*, and *intent* tends to paralyze people. For this reason, we go through this step very quickly, in minutes rather than hours and days, to sketch out the goals that will focus how we use our 100 marbles. We do this by first looking forward to identify the kind of future we want to create; then looking back from this future to the present so we can prune extraneous options from our path; and finally looking into our hearts to check how well our logic syncs up with our emotions.

## LOOK FORWARD TO FIND THE "LEAD-DOG" OBJECTIVE

We start our process of sketching out our Big Goals by looking forward to kinds of futures we could create. First we make a fast laundry list of the possible goals, without any sorting or censoring. Then we sort our list quickly by importance, so we can see which objectives should be the "lead dogs" and get most of our 100 marbles, and which ones are secondary or tertiary in importance and therefore should get fewer.

Even for very important issues, we do this first iteration very quickly. Again, our experience is that people become paralyzed when asked about their Big Goals; we do too. Doing a first draft fast forces us to get something down on paper, which gets us over the paralysis hump. We know that these drafts will be imperfect. We also know that we can then revise and refine them as we go through the remainder of this step and the rest of the Gambler's Dozen. The point is: we have to get started. You do too. Here's how.

## Create a Quick Laundry List

Start with the area of your business, or your life, on which you want to focus and take a few moments to list all the objectives you have or think you may have in this area—a kind of laundry list of possible goals. The key here is: go fast, don't try to put your thoughts in any kind of order, and don't censor. Just create your list.

Had General McClellan decided to do this, the first draft of his laundry list of objectives at Antietam might have looked like this:

- Win this battle
- Keep War Department guys in Washington happy; also Lincoln
- Follow the rules
- Don't screw up
- BEAT LEE!!!!!
- Be a hero
- Be seen as the hero—even better than Lee
- End the war
- Get a hot bath and clean clothes; burn battle underwear
- Run for President in 1864/win

When you create your own laundry list of objectives, either by yourself or with a group, your first draft may look a lot like our imaginary list for General McClellan, and have multiple and possibly somewhat conflicting objectives at all different levels of importance—and, in fact, we expect it probably will. Initial lists like this are also almost always the case for start-up companies, and particularly for technology-based start-ups, which usually have more ambition and ideas than they have time and money.

Managers and board members of such companies already know they want to get to a liquidity event, either by doing a big IPO or by being acquired. The Big Goals task for these companies is therefore to envision what their companies will have to look like in order to get to the kind of liquidity event they desire. Many start-up companies don't tackle this issue early enough in their histories, and pay the price later in time and money wasted on nonessential bets. One company that did tackle this issue in time was Cytyc Corporation.

Today, Cytyc (CYTC on the Nasdaq) is a highly successful and profitable diagnostics-products company specializing in women's healthcare. In the late 1980s, Cytyc's vision was to develop a system for automated computer-image reading and analysis of Pap smears. The idea was to both improve the detection of cervical cancer and reduce the cost of reading the slides.

Two things then happened. One was that the Cytyc scientists realized that one of the main obstacles to computer imaging was the poor quality of conventional Pap smear slides. This realization led to Cytyc's invention of ThinPrep® technology, which creates slides that are clearer, more accurate, and easier to read than those made from conventional Pap smears.

The second was that Cytyc's management, and the venture capitalists who had funded the company, realized that a lot more money would be required to accomplish all the tasks then on the company's agenda. These included commercializing the ThinPrep technology, finishing the development of the automated slide-reading system, and gaining market and regulatory acceptance for the automated system, all of which were getting some of the company's attention and money and none of which were getting enough of either to be completed successfully in anywhere close to a reasonable time frame.

Given all this, a laundry list of objectives put together by the Cytyc team at the time might have looked like this:

- Save more women from cervical cancer
- Save more women from unnecessary testing due to false positives
- Finish the automated system—this is our heart and vision!!!
- More revenues! More revenues faster!
- Commercialize ThinPrep as a standalone product line
- Create an economic model that gets us to profits quickly
- Raise more money

- Raise more money without diluting the current equity holders
- Build market position before our competitors do!

Like the list we imagined for General McClellan, this one too has multiple objectives, some of which may conflict with others. It's also highly unlikely that all the objectives can be met given available resources and time constraints.

If, as with these two lists, you find that the first draft of your laundry list also has more objectives than you can reasonably expect to achieve given your resources and the constraints you face, that's probably a great time to stop and quickly think about all the items you've listed before you take your first action.

This is always true. And it's especially true in those situations in which you feel you have just been wronged and you also feel the strong urge to hit right back.

Quick response to a perceived harm is the classic problem of the flaming e-mail reply or the cutting remark sharply delivered. First you feel great. Then you may quickly find yourself having to cope with a cascade of escalating and unpleasant effects. How many e-mails, we wonder, might not have been sent and how many feuds averted by a few moments' thought on a fuller list of objectives, including those beyond telling that other bozo off? When we posed this question to a group of senior European executives from nine companies, we speculated that perhaps 10 percent of corporate e-mails fell into this category. Their instant response: the real number is probably north of 25 percent.

## Pick the Lead Dog

Some people, when asked to create their laundry lists of objectives, will list only one goal, much as we suspect Dean Kamen did when he considered the deserted-island question. In these cases, which are pretty rare in our experience, you already have your lead-dog objective, and you can skip the rest of this section.

What's far more typical is that, like the lists we imagined for

McClellan and Cytyc, your initial lists will be messy and include multiple objectives, and some of these objectives will overlap or even conflict with others on the list. Then you're back to the problem of the 100 marbles; you can't fulfill all the objectives simultaneously, or you can't fulfill all the objectives in equal measure and still end up with the future you desire. Using your marbles wisely becomes a lot easier once you've figured out which goal or goals are the lead dogs, the ones that are most important to you and therefore the ones that you will want to give a disproportionate share of your marbles.

The McClellan and Cytyc examples illustrate the dilemma of more potential objectives than resources to invest in them. For McClellan, the constrained resource was time; he had been given the incredible gift of perfect information and perfect position, but he could use this gift to his advantage *only* if he acted fast. Then he could have won the battle and perhaps the war, but he would have had to attack without authorization from the War Department, which meant that he couldn't accomplish everything on his list in equal measure.

In the actual case, McClellan used his scarce resource to check with his bosses in Washington and complete his own customary preparations and, in the process, squandered his battlefield advantage. As to the last item on the McClellan list, in 1864 the general did run for president, as the Democratic candidate against Abraham Lincoln, to whom he lost. We wonder, had McClellan made winning at Antietam his lead-dog objective and therefore concentrated all his efforts on attacking the Confederate forces promptly, how might this have changed his and his country's histories?

For Cytyc, the key constraints were time and money; the company couldn't do everything on its list fast enough to beat its competition with the amount of money it had to invest in the effort. Instead of following the common approach of allocating a few marbles on each of the objectives and then hoping for the best, Cytyc made the very tough call to stop development of the automated computer-imaging system in order to focus fully on commercializing its ThinPrep technology. Make no mistake, for those of us involved at the beginning of Cytyc's history, Eileen included, this was an extremely difficult decision. It was also a decision that allowed the company to survive, do a successful IPO, grow to close to a $3 billion market cap in 2004, and expand its product offerings—including, at long last, a Cytyc automated computer-imaging system, which was approved by the FDA in June 2003.

The importance of identifying the lead-dog objectives holds true for career bets and life bets as well as for business bets. Take divorce as an example. People going through divorces frequently have multiple and sometimes ultimately conflicting objectives. If you feel you are the aggrieved party, what's more important to you: starting your life over, maximizing your settlement, or punishing your no-good, lying, cheating rat of a spouse for eternity? What about allowing your kids, and your kids' relationships to you and to your spouse, to survive the divorce process in a reasonably healthy way? These are all different goals, and for some separating spouses, they are mutually incompatible goals as well. Depending on which you choose, you will create different outcomes for the process itself (including how long it will take) and ultimately for your life and your kids' lives.

Or take the circumstance where you need to do something unpleasant and, at the same time, you want to be kind or helpful. On the unpleasant-task side, say you have determined that you need to fire someone, or you see a lawsuit looming that you want to stay out of despite someone else's desire to get you involved. On the desire-to-be-helpful side, say you think of yourself as a nice person and you genuinely enjoy helping others. If you aren't clear in your own mind about your primary goal, you may find that you botch both efforts— the negative task (firing the subordinate, staying out of the lawsuit) and the positive task (coaching someone who is struggling, providing support to a friend).

The lesson goes back to the principle of the 100 marbles: ranking objectives gives power. Sometimes merely identifying what you believe will give you the most future satisfaction allows you to quickly decide which bets are going to be the most important for you to take now, and which you need to avoid because they will reduce your odds of achieving your lead objective.

# LOOK BACKWARD TO PRUNE
# EXTRANEOUS OPTIONS

There's a problem with seeing your lead-dog objective and then stopping there—you can get overwhelmed by the alternative paths and options for achieving your goals.

Here's what we mean. Looking from the present to the future creates a rapidly expanding forest of potential options. Say you've chosen your lead-dog objective for a business or personal situation. Starting with where you stand today, you can delineate three or four ways you *could* proceed. Each of these alternatives in turn leads to more options that will grow out of them, another several for each. And these too will have further options. Pretty soon the options are multiplying at an alarming rate, much like the buckets in Disney's version of the Sorcerer's Apprentice. As an example, a process that has five steps with each step having 4 options will give over 1,000 options by the final step—4 options at the end of step 1 ($1\times4$), 16 options at the end of step 2 ($4\times4$), 64 options at the end of step 3 ($16\times4$), 256 options at the end of step 4 ($64\times4$), 1,024 options at the end of the final step ($256\times4$).

For many people, the resulting scope of choices is simply overwhelming. On a very prosaic level, we think this is why some people are paralyzed in mega-furniture stores that are brimming with choices; the task of making decisions in the face of so many options is more than their brains can accommodate.

But, if you plan backward from the achievement of your Big Goals back to where you are today, you can cut out many of these potential options. Dean Kamen planned back from the objective of getting off the island; that meant he could delete any potential option that wasn't going to help him meet that goal. If you know that you want your house to be comfortable, kid-friendly, and easy to keep in somewhat working order, you can probably rule out spending time in the Louis XIV department at your local home-furnishings superstore.

Similarly, when a start-up company decides that commercializing a particular product based on a particular technology is its lead-dog objective, it can use backward planning to quickly focus its efforts and prune extraneous options. If, like Cytyc, you plan to bring a new product to the market that will need FDA approval, you will have to work back through the steps of how you will distribute the product, then to how you will manufacture it, then to a working prototype, and finally back to the product specs, all in compliance with FDA standards. You'll also have to add other steps to the path, working back from an FDA approval, to completion of the scientific studies, then to selection of the sites for the research, then to the study design, then to the core scientific group you will work with.

The power of this kind of backward mapping comes after you get a sense of the whole path. Once you can see the broad outline of the path from start to finish, you can begin eliminating options at the beginning of the process that you can now see won't lead you where you want to go.

For example, you might see certain scientists and certain research options that, while interesting, won't help you with the kinds of studies you will need to do; out they go. Or you might realize that several outsourcing alternatives that had looked promising because they would give you lower costs aren't worth further pursuit because they won't meet the FDA manufacturing specifications. *Every option you prune at the beginning of the path allows you to cut all the multiple future alternatives that would have grown from that initial possibility*; the more alternatives you correctly cut, the more time and money you save, and the easier it will be for you to see whether you really want to live with the Big Goals you have chosen, given the choices they will entail—or whether you want to change your goals.

Of course, where you set your looking-back point will also make a big difference in what objective you select as your lead-dog objective. Consider the matter of weddings and marriages.

The average American wedding in 2004 cost something on the order of $22,000, which means there are a bunch that cost even more, many significantly more. If you plan back from the milestone of the wedding itself, you will have an enormous number of options for settings, decor, dresses, flowers, menus, attendants, guests, and gifts.

Now, consider what happens if you shift your betting horizon a bit farther out—say, to the early years of your marriage. For example, what if your (very generous) parents and parents-in-law have offered you the following choice:

|          Option 1          |     OR     |          Option 2          |
| --- | --- | --- |
| • $5,000 for the wedding and<br>• $50,000 for a down payment on a new house | | • $50,000 for the wedding of your dreams and<br>• nothing for a new house |

Which option would you choose? What if both of you are really into planning a boffo wedding, or only one of you is and the other finds the process tedious and irritating? What if all your friends have had big, elaborate weddings?

Part of how you answer these questions will depend on whether you've chosen your wedding day or, say, your fifth anniversary as your looking-back point. Depending on the time horizon, you may shift your choice of your lead-dog objective—the scope of the wedding itself or your economic circumstances in the early years of your marriage—and therefore how you evaluate the relative attractiveness of the bets you could place.

## LOOK FOR THE EMOTION LOOPS

In the parallel universe in which economists, consultants, and business writers live, objectives are based on pure economic choices, pure economic choices are based on quantifiable and comparable goals, and decisions are rational. In the world of poets, playwrights, and storytellers of all stripes, humans bring emotions and psychic baggage to every decision. If you want to understand your real objectives, stick with the poets, and include a look at your emotional drivers as well as at the rational goals you think you want to achieve.

Being able to see your emotional and psychic needs is important because the more vital these needs are to you, the more of your 100 marbles you will invest in their satisfaction, even to the detriment of your stated goals or your own best interests or both. We think of these kinds of actions as "emotion loops," persistent habits of behavior aimed at satisfying some set of emotional or psychic needs.

From what we can tell, there is almost an infinite variety of such emotion loops. Many of them share a common characteristic: they pull you back to some prior time or prior goal—to make up for past slights or errors, for example, or to prove something to others—or to avoid an unpleasant task. Whatever their origins, emotion loops can swamp the rational objectives you tell yourself or others you are pursuing.

What about you? Do you find yourself in an emotion loop from time to time that makes you want to be the most impressive person in some respect—the wittiest, the smartest, the most irreverent? The kindest, the wisest, the most compassionate? The least visible person in the room, the one who can't be blamed for anything? Did you take a particular point of view at some point in the past and now want to show people that you were right? Is there a problem looming on the horizon that you would just as soon not tackle? What makes you feel competent, or keeps you from feeling incompetent? What do you pretend—and why? What do you fear?

These questions can be unpleasant to address. But your answers are important because gut goals can be surprisingly strong, able to hijack other, more rational motivations. In start-up companies, for example, it is not uncommon to see entrepreneurs with high needs to maintain control and, if they are scientists or technologists, also to prove that they are the most brilliant in their fields. Sometimes they are so driven by these motivations that they forfeit economic gain for themselves and their investors in favor of maintaining control and proving their points—which is why some venture capitalists move quickly, sometimes wisely and sometimes not, to remove inventors-founders from the helms of companies they fund. (The VCs call this "founder redeployment." The founders often have other names for it.) Other times, board members avoid dealing with the problem because they find it too messy or unpalatable to be addressed directly.

All of us have emotional needs and psychic baggage. To the extent we can recognize how these needs can commandeer our rational goals, the more we can control them. If any of the preceding questions gave you a little ping as you read them, please pay attention. If you are willing to look into your heart to understand your emotion-driven motivations, you can begin to decide if these objectives are the ones you want to dominate your agenda. And, if you can understand someone else's, you can predict what they will do, sometimes better than they can themselves, which will always give you an advantage as you structure your own bets.

* * * *

For any bet, you have the equivalent of only 100 marbles to invest. The better you understand, at the beginning of your betting process, the future you are trying to create, and why you think you will be satisfied with this future once you have achieved it, the more wisely you will use the marbles you have to invest—the first step in making your own luck.

# THE DEMENTED GENIE

*You are a scientist, and you find a lamp washed up on the beach. You rub it, and out pops a genie, just like in the children's fairy tales.*

*This genie is a little different than the ones you have read about, since this genie had previously earned an MBA from Stanford. So instead of giving you three wishes about anything, this genie gives you one wish only, focused only on your career, and tells you that you can only give directional instructions about what you would like.*

*Fair enough, you figure. You ask that your scientific work be very successful financially and very widely recognized.*

*Done. You win the Lasker Prize, one of the most important prizes in medicine. Your work is also the basis for a new company that takes off and introduces products that help patients in exactly the way you had hoped. In addition to your recognition as the founder/scientist, you net $10 million after taxes when the company is sold to a large pharmaceutical firm.*

*As it turns out, though, your genie is also a little demented. As a parallel event, the genie arranges for your scientific rival—a person whom you detest as egotistical, overbearing, possibly not totally ethical, and certainly not as bright as you—to receive the Nobel Prize in medicine and to net $20 million after taxes on the company founded on the basis of his or her science.*

*Are you happy?*


*Write the first answer that came to your mind here:*

_____

# The Gambler's Dozen, Step 2

# UPSIDE/DOWNSIDE:
# Calculate Your (Potential) ROI

# Shock and Horror in the Lone Star State

"UNPRECEDENTED and unthinkable."

That was the assessment made by Thomas J. Falk, CEO of Dallas-based diaper giant Kimberly-Clark, about the behavior of archrival Procter & Gamble.

K-C's decision to raise the price of its diapers by 5 percent in the summer of 2002 must have seemed like a good idea at the time. In the United States alone there are something on the order of fifteen billion disposable diapers consumed a year. At the time of Falk's shock, K-C and its Huggies brand held about 45 percent of this market, P&G and its Pampers brand held about 35 percent, and each was bringing in a billion or two dollars in sales, plus or minus. So in the summer of 2002, when K-C hiked its prices, Falk and his colleagues at Kimberly-Clark may have assumed that they had given P&G at least fifty million good reasons to follow their lead.

But that wasn't the game that P&G decided to play. Instead of meeting K-C's price increase, the folks at Procter didn't take the increase, and then invested heavily in promotions and coupons to the consumers. The result: increases in market share and bottom-line numbers for Procter, declines in both for Kimberly-Clark.

As Falk later lamented in a front-page *Wall Street Journal* story, "We didn't expect them to take a 15 percent price reduction on Pampers for five months."

But P&G's CEO, A. G. Lafley, had been a pretty predictable character. Since his accession to CEO in 2000, Lafley relentlessly called on P&G to cut costs and "get market share and sales growing again by winning with the consumer." And, in any case, anyone who has ever worked for P&G or for one of its competitors knows that you challenge P&G on price at your own peril unless you are sure that you have the cost position and cash reserves to control the battle.

Why was Mr. Falk surprised?

# 2. Upside/Downside: Will This Game Be Worth Playing, for Me?

ANY future result you desire—large or small, corporate or personal—requires you to place bets. The question is, *do these bets represent a game you are going to want to play* in terms of what you can gain, what you can lose, and who will control the rules?

Kimberly-Clark's bet on pricing provides one slant on that question. Doug Corrigan, one of the last of the pioneer daredevil pilots from the early days of aviation, provides another.

In 1938, flying solo across the Atlantic was still new and still dangerous. So in July of that year, when the authorities turned down Corrigan's application to fly from New York to London, they were probably right.

First, in addition to the inherent danger, there was Corrigan's plane, a single-engine Curtiss-Robin. Curtiss-Robins had welded steel fuselages and wooden wings, and except for the engine cowlings, were entirely covered in fabric. Corrigan had purchased his second-hand for a bit over $300 in 1929, and then had souped up his flying crate with another $600 worth of stuff and innumerable hours tinkering, including replacing the original 90-horsepower Curtiss OX-5 engine with a secondhand 168-horsepower Wright J6-S engine.

Then there were the pilots. Or pilot. Corrigan's plane had room only for him. At cruising speeds of no more than one hundred miles an hour, Corrigan could look forward to at least twenty-four hours in the air without a radio or human companion to keep him awake. On his flight from California to New York, which took him twenty-seven hours at his cruising speed of eighty-five miles an hour, Corrigan's remedy was just to stick his head out of the cockpit window whenever he got sleepy.

And finally, there was the flight path. Going across the country, there was plenty of farm land and a chance of survival in the case of an emergency landing. Flying across the Atlantic, there would be only water—and certain death for Corrigan if he or his plane failed.

In light of all this, the only permit the authorities were willing to consider was for Corrigan to take his plane and fly back to California, and that's what they granted him. The morning of his flight back west, onlookers watched as Corrigan turned over the propeller himself, latched the cockpit door with bailing wire to a nail where a knob had once been, and, when last seen before he vanished into the clouds, headed his plane *east*. Twenty-eight hours later, when he landed at Ireland's Baldonnel Airport, Corrigan claimed that he had been following the wrong end of the magnetic compass needle in his plane, though he did note, "I thought there was an awful lot of water down there." That was his story, and that was the story he stuck to until the end of his life in 1995 at age eighty-eight.

*   *   *   *

Understanding the game you will have to play and whether playing this game is likely to be worth it *to you*, according to *your* standards and values, is the second skill of Predictive Intelligence and is the skill on which this step of the Gambler's Dozen is based. This again is an OO—Orient and Organize—skill, with particular emphasis on the first O.

This is also an underrated skill, and we find the Upside/Downside step of the Gambler's Dozen is often neglected, even by very educated people. One might have expected that Kimberly-Clark, with its army of MBAs, would have done a lot better at this step than a crackpot aviator. In our view, the reverse was true. Here's how we figure it.

In Kimberly's case, the pricing bet in 2002 was one encounter in an ongoing contest. Perhaps K-C had been blinded by the upside of a fast $50 million or more direct to the bottom line. Whatever the reason, Falk's shock at P&G's response indicates to us that while he and his colleagues may have looked hard at the upside, they seem to have overlooked the other two dimensions. On the downside, they appear to have underestimated the risk that Procter would see K-C's price increase as an opportunity for P&G to hold prices and add promotions and coupons in a bid for added market share. And on the game's rules, they appear to have misunderstood that even though they had always been the price setter for the disposable diaper category, for this encounter it was P&G that could, and did, take control of how the game would be played.

Doug Corrigan, on the other hand, did a great job on this step of the Gambler's Dozen, if you look at the situation from his perspective—and not necessarily yours or ours. The evidence is that Corrigan fully understood that the downside of his unauthorized flight was that he could lose his life. In fact, when a famous female aviator of the time, Ruth Nichols, offered to lend him a parachute for his supposed trip back to California, he declined, explaining that there was no room for it, and anyway "that the plane was all he had and if it fell to pieces he would go with it." For Corrigan, this downside was worth the risk because of his love of flying and the high value he assigned to the upside of fulfilling his life's dream of flying solo across the Atlantic. He also clearly understood the current rules and that he could take control of them, simply by getting a permit to fly somewhere else, winding the propeller, hopping into the cockpit, and then going where he wanted to go.

The aim at this step of the Gambler's Dozen is to assess your own understanding of the game you are about to enter. We do this by looking at three dimensions: the prizes and how high the upsides can be; the costs and how low the downsides can be; and the rules and who can control and change them. To the extent you can, you also want to understand these three dimensions from the perspectives of the other players as a way to enhance your ability to predict their next moves. Then you can decide—*is this game worth it to me, or should I go back to step 1 and shift my goals?*

(Incidentally, things didn't go too badly for Corrigan after he landed in Ireland. The newspapers, which had been following the mystery flight that had headed east rather than west and had not been heard from since, had a field day when the daredevil flyer finally reappeared, crowning him Wrong Way Corrigan after a reporter who, when he reached Corrigan by phone at the Irish airfield, kept shouting, "You flew the wrong way! You flew the wrong way!" The U.S. authorities suspended Corrigan's license for only the time it took for him and his plane to return to America via ocean liner. Back at home, he became a celebrity, met President Roosevelt, was feted by a massive ticker-tape parade in New York, and became the star of newsreel reports shown in movie houses of the time. And, to the end, most of all Doug Corrigan loved flying and he loved his Curtiss-Robin.)

## UPSIDES FIRST: COUNTING UP

It's fun to count your chickens before they hatch—we like to count our chickens even before the eggs have been laid. How much of human progress would never have been achieved if dreamers and idealists and entrepreneurs and movers and shakers had never counted up what they could gain from an adventure even before they had figured out the first steps to get there?

So when we start thinking about whether a game will be worth it to us, we count up and look at the upside first, before we count down and figure out what the potential costs could be. There's an important reason for this, in addition to our personal preferences. If you don't understand the upsides first, you may not ever see the opportunity cost of delay or inaction.

At Antietam, would General McClellan have made better decisions for himself and for the country if he had understood the opportunity cost of delay, once he knew, for as close to certain as we get in this life, that his troops were *at that moment* in position to win the battle decisively and thus end the war—but only if he acted fast and bypassed customary military protocols? If so, we suspect that

McClellan could only have taken such action if he had looked at this upside first, before looking at the downside of acting without full approvals. Otherwise, after analyzing the potential negatives, he might never have gotten to the point of even asking how big the gains on the upside might be.

It can also be highly useful to understand the upsides from the other guy's point of view. Had Falk and the other managers at Kimberly-Clark looked at the upsides from P&G's perspective, they might have understood that P&G was defining its upside in line with Lafley's goal of "getting market share and sales growing again by winning with the consumer." By that definition, holding its list prices and adding promotions and coupons to gain market share and sales provided a better upside for them than going for a price increase that would add to the bottom line but not move the needle on share or unit sales.

And then there is the issue of looking at the upsides first for the purpose of avoiding getting locked into a W. C. Fields type of game, the kind in which even the best outcomes aren't appealing to you.

W. C. Fields was a 1920s film star and comic, and he didn't like Philadelphia. So his joke was a contest for which first prize would be a week in Philadelphia, and second prize would be . . . two weeks in Philadelphia. If you also aren't partial to Philadelphia, after you've gotten the news about the upsides for the winners and runners-up, the additional information that the losers will have to spend, say, *three* weeks in Philadelphia doesn't add any useful information to your evaluation *because you already know you don't want to play.* Once you've figured out that you lose even if you succeed, learning how much more pain the downside holds is not going to make this game more attractive to you.

There are lots of games that fit the W. C. Fields mold for some people and not for others. For Doug Corrigan, the prospect of flying across the Atlantic solo for twenty-eight hours with no heat, no toilet, no sleep, and precious little of anything else was pure heaven; for many of the rest of us, you couldn't pay us enough to endure what he did even if you could guarantee our success.

The same is true of jobs. Some people look at the range of tasks of being a chef-owner of a gourmet restaurant as part of the upside of such a venture; others would see everything except for the net cash cleared each week as part of the downside. If you are offered a job that has great pay and requires at least two weeks of overseas travel per month, is that an upside for you or a downside? What if the travel is all first class?

People look at such situations with different perspectives and values, and what may seem to be an attractive game with great upsides to one person may be regarded as a W.C. Fields game to another. Your task is to decide which it is for you, by your values. If your assessment is that even in the best of circumstances, you don't much like the upsides and you don't think you will be able to grab control of the rules to change the prizes, then just looking at the upsides may already have given you enough information for you to determine that this game is not worth playing, for you.

## DOWNSIDES SECOND: COUNTING DOWN

As much as we like counting chickens, we know that where there are chickens, there are also foxes, hawks too. And where there could be hawks, it's prudent to look at the downsides before making decisions about whether to play this game or go back and revise objectives.

In plain-vanilla stock market investing and casino gambling, the downsides are usually fairly straightforward. You put your money and time in, and you can lose everything you're about to spend. If your style of stock market investing is to buy on margin or sell short, then your potential downside is a lot bigger—everything you've put in plus a lot more if you bet wrong.

The big question is, what can you *stand to lose*? It's important to be clear here. There are huge differences between losing what you consider to be a manageable amount of money, and losing more: losing all your money, going into debt, wasting five years of your life, destroying friendships, losing your reputation, going to jail, or risking your life. There is risk in everything, of course, but the first step in assessing the downside of any game is knowing what kind of assets you will be risking and how much of each.

People who are very educated or very successful or both often glide over the question of how much they could lose and whether it is more than they can stand. Often this is because their talents and past successes lead them to believe that they will be able to navigate around any downsides. Perhaps that's what happened to Martha Stewart, convicted in 2004 on four felony charges related to an ImClone stock trade she had completed at the end of 2001 and on which she had gained a grand total of $52,000.

As we go over the story, we wonder how Stewart looked at the downsides of the various options she had after her ImClone trade hit the news. She could have, as one option, been totally open with the investigators early, before charges, if any, were filed, and negotiated for a small punishment if and as necessary. The downsides of this option would have included the possibility of admitting publicly to some form of an error or wrongdoing, and perhaps having to agree to a plea on an agreed set of charges. This would have been embarrassing, but we guess that it wouldn't have involved jail time and, though it might have entailed some hit to her reputation, that the public relations damage would have been minor and relatively easy to repair.

A second set of options would have been to wait until the prosecutor took action and then to agree to a plea bargain based on the government's case. It was widely reported that Stewart had received at least two proposals of this type. Though the terms of the two proposals differed, both reportedly would have allowed Stewart to avoid a trial and allowed her to continue working at her company in exchange for copping a plea to one of the felony charges and paying a fine. Both also reportedly would have come with a prosecution recommendation of no jail time, which, while not a guarantee, would have given her very high odds of avoiding prison.

The third option, and the one Stewart chose, was to go for broke and stand trial, betting that she could beat the charges. The upside on this choice, if she got the not-guilty verdicts she was hoping for, was that she would be exonerated, her brand name would be easier to rehabilitate, and she wouldn't have to deal with any restrictions on corporate activities that could come with a felony conviction.

The downsides of going to trial were that Stewart was risking most or everything she had accumulated up to that point as well as everything she could leverage to create future personal assets. These included: a personal net worth of over $300,000,000; her golden brand name that had the potential of generating future additional hundreds of millions of dollars; and her continued participation in the company that she had founded and nurtured.

At the same time, the prosecution's upsides and downsides also changed when Stewart elected to go to trial. When an accepted plea bargain is in place, prosecutors don't have to worry about the downside of losing a high-profile and very visible case. But once there's no plea bargain, both the upsides and downsides for the prosecutors become much bigger and so do the prosecutors' motives to do everything in their power to win.

Now put yourself in Stewart's situation. Even if you had Stewart's skill of making the best of a bad situation, given the upsides and downsides for you and for the prosecution under each of these sets of options, what estimate of the odds of getting convicted would have gotten you to shift from going for broke to one of the settlement options? One in two? One in four? One in ten? One in a hundred?

As a matter of general principle, if the upside is what you would like to come to pass and you don't see much downside, you may be underestimating the potential costs of the game you are thinking of entering. In these cases, forcing yourself to think about the downsides and what your life would be like if they came to pass is a highly useful exercise. And if you understand how other people in the same game assess their downsides, you may be able to see ways to use this information to play more wisely and thereby up your odds of making the game work to your benefit.

# THEN . . . CHECK THE RULES

The last piece of figuring out the potential value to you of entering a game is to understand the rules and the rulemakers. Understanding the current rules allows you to begin to estimate the odds of where on the continuum of upsides and downsides your outcomes will fall *if* the rules stay the same. Understanding who does or could control the rules allows you to forecast how these rules could change and whether these changes are likely to work for or against your interests.

In some cases, just knowing what the rules and who the rulemakers are will tell you enough that you can easily forecast the most likely outcomes. That's what former Senator Bill Bradley found after his encounter with the butter man at a formal dinner.

The story, as Howard heard Bradley tell it, is that when the butter man came to Bradley, he put one pat of butter on Bradley's bread plate. Bradley politely asked for a second pat. And the server said: No. Bradley, somewhat shocked, turned to the butter man and said: Do you know who I am? And the server said: No. Bradley then told him: I am the guest of honor here tonight, and I am the speaker. I am a United States senator, and I am running for president of the United States. I was an NBA all-star, and before that I was All-American in basketball from Princeton. And the server looked at Bradley for a few seconds and then responded: Do you know who I am? Bradley said he did not. To which the server responded: I am the man in charge of the butter. Bradley didn't get the extra pat.

In some ways, Martha Stewart was in a similar situation when she chose to go to trial. Plea bargains are relatively certain; judges can change the terms but usually don't. But with a trial, Stewart was putting her fate in the hands of new rulemasters, not only the judge but now also a jury—none of whom, it may be reliably assumed, had net worths of $300,000,000 or could even imagine the kind of life in which a person could hop on a private jet, make a stop, call her broker and net a quick $52,000, have her jet refueled, and go on to some lavish resort. Like the butter man, the members of the jury on Martha

Stewart's case may not have had her privileges, but they sure controlled the butter.

In that respect, when Stewart chose to go to trial, she was also making a predictable and definable shift in who would control the rules, from a mutual agreement with the prosecutors and approval by the judge to full control by the judge and jury. In other games, a shift occurs when one player seizes control of the rules after the play has begun. That's what Corrigan did after the authorities gave him a permit to fly back to California and he headed his plane east rather than west after takeoff. And that's what P&G did to Kimberly-Clark when it didn't raise its prices after K-C's price increase.

Certainly, even though K-C had been the longstanding price leader in the disposable diaper category, Procter's move was neither "unthinkable" nor "unprecedented." For one thing, just because a company has been the price leader doesn't mean it will continue to be. And for another, P&G's behavior and words for some time had indicated that it was more interested in gaining share than in higher per-unit prices.

In fact, P&G had had a persistent, clear, and public message that it was out to gain share and grow revenues in all categories, including disposable diapers. In addition, P&G had twice moved to lower its diaper prices on the premium Baby Stages portion of its lineup in the several months before K-C's 2002 price increase. And, in any case, in the world of packaged goods, the Procter army has been renowned for decades for its disciplined approach to winning. Given all this, Procter's move to grab control of the game and its rules as soon as Kimberly-Clark provided an opportunity for P&G to do so was at least feasible, if not absolutely predictable.

When it comes to the rules, it's important to remember that even when you've been in control, other people may turn out to be better players. Great players may even change the game. Do you think you are playing golf or soccer? Does the low score win, or the high score? Just because you show up with a white sphere and ready to play doesn't mean that the rules by which you played (and, perhaps, won) the game yesterday will be the rules by which you will have to play the game tomorrow. Your job, at this step in the Gambler's Dozen, is to assess who could take and keep control of the rules, and how this will affect the likely upsides and downsides of the game you are planning to enter.

\*  \*  \*  \*

People and companies differ, of course, on what they see as attractive balances between possible upsides, downsides, and control of the rules. It's hard for either of us to imagine ourselves as generals in the middle of bloody, terrible battles, as McClellan was or as daredevil pilots with nailed-together flying crates. Neither of us would likely have taken the risks that Corrigan did, and both of us hope that we would have been bold enough to have attacked quickly at Antietam once we were reasonably certain that the enemy plans now in our hands were accurate and current.

No matter how we differ though, all smart bettors share the same task at this step of the Gambler's Dozen: to invest our 100 marbles where the balance between upsides, downsides, and control of the rules looks most attractive, according to our preferences and assessments. The converse is true too—to the extent we can, we never want to waste our marbles when the likely downsides outweigh the upsides, or the rules are or could easily be controlled by people whose interests don't match ours or even run counter to ours. In those cases our advice is, stop, go back to step 1 and invent a different game where you will be better able to make your own luck.

## THE HAPPY HANDYMAN

*An adult son is visiting his father and mother, who are reno-
vating their home. As the son walks up the driveway, he notices the truck of the electrician his parents have hired. The
door of the truck is open, and inside he notices a large sign in
the cab of the truck.*

*The sign says:*

They work. We play.
They're rich. We're happy.

*The son walks into the house, greets his parents, tells them
what he has seen, and recommends strongly that they pay the
electrician for the work done to date and hire someone else
for the remainder of the job.*

*If you were his father or mother, what would you do, and
why?*

___ *Change to a new electrician*

___ *Stick with the current electrician*

# The Gambler's Dozen, Step 3

# JUMP BETS:
# Assess the Need to Make a
# Radical Shift, Right Now

# Listen My Children and You Shall Hear

AS the colonists saw it, the British were up to no good.

It was April in Boston, 1775, and local leaders had, as Paul Revere later recounted, "formed ourselves into a Committee for the purpose of watching the Movements of the British soldiers." Interactions between the colonists and the British had been peaceful, relatively speaking, but still the colonists were wary.

Ten miles to the north and west of Boston lay Lexington, where two other colonist leaders, Samuel Adams and John Hancock, were in residence for a meeting of the Massachusetts Provincial Congress. Ten miles beyond that was Concord, where local militias had stored guns and ammunition. Rumors swirled about possible British plans to march from Boston to Lexington to arrest Adams and Hancock, and then onto Concord to seize the munitions.

The colonists understood that the timing of a shift in their own behavior to thwart the British would be crucial. Too early, and the British would change their attack plans; too late, and the colonists would be dealt a massive blow. The British knew this too, and for that reason the British military governor of Massachusetts didn't even tell his officers about the assault until the last minute. So the colonists waited and watched, looking for anything out of the ordinary.

On Saturday, April 15, the British seemed to be paying less attention to routine patrols and more to their boats. Tuesday, April 18, brought other changes in British behavior: unusual numbers of officers on Boston's wharves, whispering; increased activity around the harbor; sailors on shore running errands; and, later that evening, soldiers marching. By ten o'clock that night, the new pattern seemed clear enough to sound the alarm, and Paul Revere was dispatched on his famous midnight ride (later celebrated in the Longfellow poem that begins, "Listen my children and you shall hear / Of the midnight ride of Paul Revere").

Early the next day, when the British troops, over 600 strong, arrived in Lexington, they were greeted, to their shock, by a group of 38 armed men ready to fight; then onto Concord that same morning where they were met by 450 armed rebels who, now better organized, fought back effectively, inflicted heavy casualties, and pushed the British back to Boston.

And with these two battles began the American Revolutionary War. Would Canada now be twice its present size had the colonists *not* been willing to make a radical jump when they saw the British deviate from their normal patterns?

# 3. Jump Bets: Do I Need to Make a Radical Shift Now?

SOMETIMES, no matter how well you plan, you may sense an important or unexpected shift in how things have been going and find yourself with only a short amount of time to decide whether to stay the course or jump to a new path. The third skill of Predictive Intelligence is being able to see these unexpected turning points early enough and act quickly enough that you don't miss the best window for revising your bets.

Paul Revere and his fellow colonists needed this skill in 1775 and, two centuries and several decades later, a mutual fund manager based in Boston found himself in a similar kind of situation.

The venue was an investor meeting for a technology company in which the fund manager had enthusiastically invested. This day, though, things began to go wrong almost from the time he stepped into the room.

First, there was the business of the two IRs. As this investor saw it, one investor relations professional is standard operating procedure. Two was one too many and could only mean too much to explain.

Then there were the executives themselves. They had nice tans. But the company's headquarters were in the northeast United States, and it was winter. Whatever these guys had been doing, it didn't look like it involved much work at the home office. Strike two.

And finally there were the speeches. Midway through the first one, one of the tanned execs began to describe company plans to "reconfigure the software for a new platform."

Our friend the mutual fund manager, who was sitting in the rear of the room, says he didn't know what that meant—but, whatever it was, he was "pretty sure it wasn't good." So he immediately slipped out the back, while the first exec was still talking, got the trading floor on the phone, and began unloading his shares as fast as he could.

As it turned out, he didn't sell exactly at the peak, but he got out in time to lock in a big chunk of his gain. The company—and the investors who hung in with it—didn't fare as well. The share price tanked, much of the workforce was laid off, and the remaining assets were bought up at a fraction of the high water mark for the stock.

* * * *

Paths to the future seldom run smooth. Whatever your goals—to bring forth a new nation, conceived in liberty; or to make your investors money, consistently (and more money than they could earn with one of your competitors); or even to host a successful dinner party—you may sense that the situation around you is unfolding differently than you anticipated. Then you might find yourself at a potential turning point with only a limited time to decide whether to keep on as you had planned or shift to a new path. Making that radical shift in premises and action in a short amount of time is what we call a *jump bet*.

Spotting the unexpected turning points fast enough to catch the opportunity for an attractive jump bet is the skill on which this step is based. This is primarily an OO—Orient and Organize—skill, because the earlier you see the need to consider a jump bet, the more able you will be to reorient and reorganize your thinking to take advantage of the turning point—to grab a new and unexpected opportunity or to reduce exposure to a new and unexpected downside—*while* the window for this bet remains open.

Since the idea of jump bets isn't standard-issue business strategy, this chapter begins with a short explanation of what we mean when we talk about jump bets, and why we put the skill of seeing these bets early in the OOPA! process. Then we move to the mechanics of scanning the horizon for clues that an unexpected turning point may be at hand and assessing whether to jump or stay the course when you only have a short time to decide and then to act.

## LIFE, LIBERTY, AND THE PURSUIT OF JUMP BETS

Jump bets are a way gamblers with high PIs take advantage of unexpected changes. Instead of seeing signs that usual behaviors and causal relationships may be shifting and then waiting until the whole new pattern unfolds, high-PI gamblers jump *before* all the information is in so they can grab opportunities that they estimate won't be available later or only will be available at much higher prices.

Jump bets as we define them have two distinctive characteristics. First, they are disruptive in some way—they may be unexpected, or expected but not at this time, but in all cases they require a change in the way you are used to doing things or in the way you were planning to do things in the future. And second, they come with relatively brief windows for acting and taking advantage of the changes in the world around you. Little jump bets have small consequences in terms of opportunities gained or lost. Big jump bets have relatively big consequences.

McClellan faced a big jump bet when his troops found the Lost Order at Antietam; so did Paul Revere and his fellow rebels once they became convinced that a preemptive attack by the British was imminent. Our friend the mutual fund manager also faced a jump bet, though of smaller magnitude, when he saw a handful of small anomalies that made him worry that the worst was yet to come for one of the equities in his portfolio.

The question is, if a new pattern is forming in an area of importance for your future, will you see it in time to make a jump bet that improves your odds, before the window closes? Brief windows mean quick decisions—either to change course or continue as previously planned—even when the potential consequences are huge. People who can see these turning points, and are willing to place their jump bets in time, can up their odds of protecting their current positions or gaining on their competitors; they can appear on Lexington Green to prevent the British troops from arresting Adams and Hancock, or bail out of a stock before others begin selling and the share price plummets.

Jump bets come at a price, though, and one of these is the price of pride. When you face a jump bet, you may feel that you are acknowledging that your prior predictions, and therefore your judgment about what to do, were at least somewhat flawed and quite possibly completely wrong. The more your self-image is deeply bound up in being seen as right and correct in all your judgments, the more this kind of acknowledgment will make you feel uneasy, or worse. Then you are in the soup; your self-concept will not let you jump and your current path won't get you where you want to go.

The problem with this is that it is *backward* thinking; you are looking *back* at your prior predictions and using your current bets to prove that your past views were correct. But betting is a *forward* activity; smart gamblers always bet based on current predictions, not past ones.

*And, in fact, predictions can and should change because what we know changes.* What we know right now may be very different and more complete than what we were able to see at an earlier time. Since today's bets need to be based on today's predictions about tomorrow, whether you were right or wrong yesterday is irrelevant to the bets you need to place at this moment, as long as you don't replicate a past mistake. Viewed from this perspective, seeing and taking a good jump bet means you were able to change your premises in time to capture better odds than you could have gotten by staying the course.

All this brings us back to Paul Revere and the "Committee for the purpose of watching the Movements of the British soldiers." Seeing the need for a jump bet starts with being open to the idea that there may be a new pattern forming and that you may have to act quickly—and with incomplete information—to take advantage of the unexpected turning point created by this new pattern.

## SCAN THE HORIZON

The best way to search for incipient opportunities or threats as they are forming is to look for bits of data that don't fit what you have come to think of as the normal pattern. These are outliers in the sense that they are outside of what you expect to see; they are important because they *may* be harbingers of a new pattern that will affect your world. You may have already seen these data bits and tucked them away in your brain as "odd" or "wrong-headed," or you may set out to search for such clues by looking back at events you had previously ignored as trivial or irrelevant.

In the diaper-wars example, the fact that P&G had tried to lower prices on part of its lineup twice in 2002 before Kimberly-Clark raised its prices a few months later was probably an important clue that P&G might not be so keen on following K-C's price increase. For Paul Revere's cohorts, it was the relative lack of attention by the British troops to their usual routines. Whatever the clues, the best way to search is not to zoom in fast and focus, but rather to fly high and float so you can see what may possibly be out of the ordinary. In this way, you are trying to be open to signals that you need to adjust the lenses you use to understand the world around you.

When we look for what might be odd (and therefore what might be an important sign), we think about two kinds of clues: the obvious ones, like the Lost Order; and the subtle, fuzzy ones, like the ones that our friend the mutual fund manager picked up on at the meeting of one of his investments. The neon clues are obvious but often ignored because they are threatening or inconvenient; the fuzzy clues are difficult to see and then ignored because they seem so insubstantial. Both, though, are critical because they represent the only advance notice we get of a jump bet that will be highly advantageous to us, but only if we see the clues and act on them before the opportunity is lost.

## Can You Deal with the Neon Clues?

Some potential jump bets are so obvious you actually have to make an effort not to see them. Even so, they are also often ignored. We think that's because of the nature of the beast: jump bets, even when they are obvious, are, by (our) definition, disruptive in some way, which means they mess up previously established schedules and operating procedures, or they require actions that go against the way we like to think about ourselves or the way we like to do things. If it's a big jump bet with a very short time fuse, you will almost certainly have to make your decision with insufficient and incomplete data and far less comfort than you would prefer.

This may have been part of what happened with General McClellan at Antietam. By all accounts he was, by preference and temperament, a thoughtful, thorough man. By virtue of getting the enemy's plans, though, he was faced with a very brief window for deciding whether to do things differently than he had intended and, as a further problem, without the full knowledge and authorization of those above him in the chain of command. And, as he was likely aware, he couldn't have it both ways: take advantage of the opportunity before Lee's troops moved to a less vulnerable configuration *and* conduct the battle as he had planned.

If you work in a large organization, the disruption of recognizing obvious clues can be an especially difficult problem; the signals may be clear, but out of sequence with annual plans and budgets. Then comes the choice: rock the boat now, or wait until the next planning cycle begins. Rocking the boat now can hurt you even if it helps the company in the long term; waiting can harm the company in the long term but have little career risk for you now or even when the threat eventually hits. This dilemma is structural, and in some ways it becomes an Achilles' heel for large enterprises.

In fact, though the Greeks who told the tale of Achilles were speaking of gods and warriors and great battles, they might as well have been speaking of modern corporate classics: the American auto industry that consistently ignored the German and Japanese imports or the big integrated steel producers around the world that consistently ignored the threats posed by the new minimills. In both these industries, there were people inside the companies who saw the dangers early on and who also felt, probably correctly, that bringing up the issue forcefully would be a CLM—career-limiting move. (We know because we've met some of those people.)

Or, going from cars to coffee, what took Procter & Gamble (Folgers) and General Foods (Maxwell House) so long to see the shift in consumer taste, from Robusta to Arabica and other gourmet beans, not just in coffee bars but also for home use? Again, there were people inside these companies who saw the shift early and who also understood the disruption of trying to address the issue now versus letting it slide by.

And, independent of size and even in personal relationships, there's another problem. This one occurs when you were one of the people who had advocated the path that you now think needs to be changed. Then you're in the uncomfortable position of trying to convince your boss (or your parent, or your spouse) to make a shift from what you had originally recommended. In these cases you may find that your judgment is impugned ("If this is the right answer, why were you telling me the opposite yesterday?") or that you are asked to prove, beyond a shadow of a doubt, that a jump bet is required.

But here's the thing: since jump bets come with short time fuses, opportunities pass and the windows for the best bets close. Those who wait for proof positive, even in the face of the neon clues, are guaranteeing that they will miss this set of jump bets. Will better bets come along? Possibly, but that's a gamble too. You may wait for more proof, and later have a less attractive selection of bets to place either because you have fewer choices or because the prices are disproportionately higher or both.

The key is, at some point, you have to bet. If you pass up the jump bet, your implicit gamble is that staying on the current path gives better odds than making the shift. Whichever way you bet, you will never know for sure, at the time you place your bet, what outcome you will achieve. Just like every other bettor, you will have to act without complete certainty about the future results.

## Can You See the Fuzzy Clues?

In other cases, the window for a jump bet opens with hardly a sound, and closes the same way. If you're a successful survivor of company layoffs, management shifts, and mergers, you are probably expert at seeing these kinds of clues which you may call "reading the tea leaves." If you've been worried about a family member—a spouse you fear may be cheating on you, a child you want to keep from falling into drugs, or a niece you want to make sure isn't being abused—then you too may be getting better and better at what you call "reading the signs." In either case, you're looking for the fuzzy clues, just as the colonists worried about unusual numbers of British officers on the wharves of Boston and our friend the fund manager worried about an extra IR at an investors meeting.

Clues like these are inferential; they depend on soft skills of instinct and intuition. They are important even though they aren't easily amenable to detailed spreadsheet analysis because we often recognize patterns on some precognitive level substantially before we can fully articulate and explain what we are seeing. A nagging feeling, a sense of an opportunity around the corner, a hunch, irritation, or even anger that the world isn't behaving as it should, all these can be signs that you are observing subtle clues that echo patterns that you have seen before.

If you find your mind wandering onto a topic that you thought was pretty well resolved, or you find yourself increasingly uneasy, ask yourself why you're thinking about these matters. Perhaps your subliminal mind is telling you that you are missing a better alternative to your planned strategy. Or if you find yourself enraged that someone has suggested that you are on the wrong path, ask yourself whether part of your reaction is that, in your heart of hearts, you fear that they may be right.

Then comes the difficult part. Once you have some of the fuzzy clues, you have to decide whether you are seeing the leading edge of a new story or just some extraneous details. Is your daughter ditching her old friends because she's begun to use drugs, or is it just the normal behavior of being a teenager? Did your boss buy a new Porsche because he's negotiating a secret sale of the company and expects a big chunk of the proceeds, or is it just the normal behavior of a middle-aged manager?

No one can give you a guaranteed answer to these questions. But the more you look, the more clues you can collect, and the more clues you have, the better able you are to see if the new clues suggest a new pattern. (Boss buys new car. Boss travels more than usual. Colleague spots Boss in New York having dinner with an investment banker. Boss seems in a better mood lately. Boss pushes harder than usual to get all revenues in this year's results and to defer as many expenses as possible. Hmmmm.)

## MAKE THE CALL: TO JUMP OR NOT TO JUMP?

The point of jump bets is once you see the turning point, you have a limited amount of time to decide to jump, or to stay the course. We can almost guarantee that you won't have enough information to *know* you are making the right decision. But still, you will have to decide and then act.

When we think our best option is to jump, we test it by speeding through the rest of the Gambler's Dozen and quickly answering, as best we can in limited time, the governing question for each of the remaining steps. We find that this is an important discipline, not only as a check on our working decision but also as a counterbalance to some of the emotions that can accompany taking a jump bet.

Sometimes there's a kind of euphoria and mass momentum toward the jump, as during the hyperbull markets around the world in 1999 and especially in the United States. That's when many previously conservative investors jumped into trading stocks with aggressive valuations, because, well, everyone else was and the markets were rising. In these cases, the investors who did best were those who resisted the euphoria and didn't jump from their traditional approaches.

More often, though, there's an emotional resistance to making the jump. People often decide to stay on the same path they've been on in the hope that with just a little more money or time or both everything will turn out as planned, which will validate all the previous investments. This kind of wishful thinking occurs even when many of the new clues suggest worse outcomes from staying the course than from walking away now—as many veterans of troubled companies, bad jobs, and deteriorating marriages can attest.

And despite all the hoopla around entrepreneurs, young companies are equally at risk for passing up good jump bets in favor of sticking with their original business plans. Heartbreak at the Start-Up Hotel could be an endless soap opera, featuring a different real-life failing company every day, and starring a whole cast of characters who fell in love with an initial business model or technology and who weren't courageous enough to read the signs from the market and adjust their strategies accordingly. Despite encountering repeated turning points, these companies turn down the jump bets and keep doing what they've been doing, even when the expected great results keep being "just around the corner," always next quarter, and never right now.

Satellite communications has been one of those technologies that investors just seem to fall in love with. Satellite Business Systems (SBS), founded in 1975 as a joint venture of Comsat, IBM, and Aetna Life and Casualty, is one example. When the company was unwound a decade later, the investors could be proud that SBS had created the first private professional satellite digital communications network. The investors also could only count their losses, because the company never created a viable economic model that could cover its costs. Ten years later, Iridium, a worldwide mobile phone and data communications system to be powered, originally, by seventy-seven low-earth-orbit satellites, did the same to its investors, but on a larger scale—something on the order of $5 billion lost before the company went into bankruptcy in 1999. In both companies, the managers and the investors faced jump bets. As with our friend the mutual fund manager, those who saw these bets early were the ones who were hurt the least.

* * * *

Jump bets are a way to adjust course and up your odds, because the earlier you can see that an emerging pattern is different from what you expected, the better able you will be to seize the new high ground and invest your 100 marbles there rather than where you had initially planned.

The problem is that jump bets are tough to see, and even tougher to act on. Most of us, most of the time, hate being disrupted. We don't like being disrupted from what we have planned to do, we don't like being disrupted from doing the things we like to do and, most of all, we don't like having to acknowledge that our prior predictions may have been wrong.

That's why it's so important to scan the environment for jump bets that may need to be taken now or shortly, inconvenient and personally unpleasant as that may be, and then, in time available, be willing to consider leaping, even given incomplete information and short time frames to decide and act. Those with high Predictive Intelligence see these opportunities and take advantage of them consistently and thereby make their own luck. Average bettors opt for keeping the security of executing according to previously set plans or continuing in paths that are comfortable and known, even when presented with the chance to jump to a better path.

Which kind of bettor are you?

## SAINT PETER SPEAKS

*A farmer turns on his radio and hears the local weather fore-cast: Torrential rains. Flooding likely. Emergency evacuation procedures in place.*

*The farmer stays put. I trust in the Lord, he says, and the Lord will save me.*

*The rains begin, and the river rises. Soon the waters are waist high in the farmer's house, and a rowboat happens by. Hop in, says the guy in the rowboat. We can get you to high ground.*

*No thanks, says the farmer. The Lord will save me.*

*And the rains continue, and the water rises up to the second floor. Then another rowboat happens by, just outside the bedroom window. We've come to get you, says the rower. Let us take you to higher ground.*

*No thank you, says the farmer. The Lord will save me.*

*Still the rains continue, and the waters rise, and the farmer climbs to the very peak of his roof. Finally a Coast Guard helicopter flies overhead, lowers a rope, and one of the crew shouts down, Get into the sling, and we'll hoist you up, and fly you to safety.*

*Thanks, no, says the farmer. The Lord will save me.*

*And the rains continue, and the waters rise further, and the farmer drowns.*

*When the farmer arrives at the Pearly Gates, he takes one look at Saint Peter, and says, What happened?!! You were supposed to save me!!!!*

*And Saint Peter says, Well, we did send you two rowboats and a helicopter.*


*If you had to make a list of the rowboats you've seen recently, including the ones you've passed up, what would be on your list? Are you willing to put your list on paper, even just for you to see?*

**The Gambler's Dozen, Step 4**

# CAMPAIGN PLANS:
Marshall Your Forces

# Square Dance of the Politicos

WERE he still alive, ballet master George Balanchine couldn't choreograph it better.

We speak of running for office in a democratic society, which almost always requires fancy footwork in a square dance, the new-world version of a quadrille, which in addition to its intricate steps comes with a caller who keeps the dance moving with a set of patter sayings ("Swing your partner, dosey doe"). We'll use the example of an American election, since that's the system we know best, and specifically of a nonincumbent running for president.

Our hypothetical candidate can anticipate that activists in both parties have strongly held views at the left and right ends of the spectrum—and that most elections will ultimately be determined by a chunk of swing voters whose views cluster around the middle, with some a bit to the right and others a bit to the left. We can therefore expect the caller for this dance to call the following steps and use the accompanying (slightly modified) traditional patter sayings.

1. Establish support with the party faithful. If you are a Democrat, slide to the left. If you are a Republican, slide to the right. *Big foot up and little foot down, Grab your own and swing 'em round.*
2. Win enough delegates to snag the nomination. Use your acceptance speech to move closer to the center. *Hold your partner, and your corner too, Now wave at the gal across from you.*

3. Settle into the White House. After a year or two, move closer to the center by co-opting the issues that the opposition party used to call its own, and start planning for reelection. *All join hands and circle wide, Spread left and right like an old cow hide.*

This is the dance Bill Clinton danced, and after him, George W. Bush. The moves may be obvious in retrospect, but in real time they seem gradual, almost imperceptible.

Now, what happens as tools like the Internet and massive electronic databases mature, and the politicians' traditional slides and sidesteps become easier to detect and broadcast widely in real time?

# 4. Campaign Plans: Who Will I Need and How Will I Get Them?

ALL objectives involve campaigns. Like a candidate seeking elected office, you up your odds when you are clear on who you will need on your side—and on how you will enlist them. If you think of this as selling, you're right. Engaging the people whose support you will need when you need it is the fourth skill of Predictive Intelligence, and it applies whether your aim is to win political office, effect organizational change, raise money for a new venture, implement a strategy at your company, or plan a family reunion.

It also applies if you are heading up a fund-raising campaign for a university. That's the position Howard found himself in when responsibility for raising capital for Harvard Business School's endowment fund was added to his academic duties. And that's when Howard and his team, thinking about what it would take to get the people whose help they would need, decided to make some radical shifts to the time-honored approach that Harvard and virtually all other U.S. colleges and universities use to identify target donors and engage their support.

Here are some of the key changes they made: They reduced the focus on the twenty-fifth reunion celebrants because twenty-five years out is precisely the time most alums are simultaneously paying college tuitions and taking care of elderly parents. They moved from giving the standard canned pitch to engaging in conversation and tailoring options based on what each prospective donor was looking for. And, perhaps most radically of all, they started every conversation by acknowledging that the school probably wasn't, and probably shouldn't be, one of the person's top three charitable priorities, but they hoped to convince the prospective donor that it should be in the next four, and explained why. And then they proceeded to break all fund-raising records at Harvard Business School, bringing in about $500 million over the course of the campaign.

The purpose of this step in the Gambler's Dozen is to lay out your plan for how you will gain the support of the people you will need in your campaign in the ways and at the times that will be most useful to you. This is the skill that Howard and his team used as they crafted their campaign to raise funds, and it's the skill you'll need as well as you organize your efforts to achieve your goals.

Many people think of selling as something "those other guys do"—politicians, that is, or fund-raisers or sales reps—and some people disparage this skill as "just" selling. Our experience tells us that just the reverse is true. The ability to sketch out a good campaign plan early in the betting process is a critical OO—Orient and Organize— skill that pays off repeatedly as you work to achieve a set of goals.

Perhaps because neither of us comes from a traditional sales background, we've crafted our approach to laying out the campaign to be quick and fun, even for people who don't think of themselves as having selling skills. First we look backward to get the whos and whens and think empathetically to figure out the hows. Then we check the tracks we will leave as we make our choices of who, when and how, or what we call the vapor trail. Political candidates go through these ministeps as they craft their campaigns, and you will need to too, regardless of your objectives.

## SKETCH OUT THE WHOS AND THINK EMPATHETICALLY TO GET THE HOWS

Before you sell, you need to identify who you need to reach. This may seem obvious, but in practice it's easy to start a campaign before you've laid out who you're going to need and when you're going to need them. Then, midway in a campaign, you find that you skipped some critical people. In that case, you will face one of the following two bad outcomes: either you will have to double back to secure the support of these folks—which eats up time and money—or you will discover that you've pretty much lost some of the people who could have helped you the most, at least for the duration of this campaign.

For this reason, we start this step with a simple list of the people, or types of people, whose support we're going to need to achieve the goals we've set for ourselves. Then we work backward to create a rough time line of when we will need each of these people's help. In the case where we see more than one distinct path to our goal, we do several backward lists of whos, one for each option. And in either case we work fast.

We start at the end and work backward because this makes it easier to see the entire group of people we will need and to put them in some sort of sequence. We work relatively quickly and *without* thinking about *how* we will get everyone on board, because otherwise we get brain cramps that block our ability to see the people who can help us, even if right now we have no idea about how to get them.

Starting with the whos and working backward is the thinking that underlies our Square Dance of the Politicos. The presidential candidates know that the desired end result requires millions of voters. But they also know that to get there, they have to start with the party loyalists and then work through a whole chain of people and challenges to raise money, win state primaries, raise more money, snag the nomination, keep raising money, and then persuade enough of the swing voters in enough states to tip the balance in the Electoral College.

This is not so different from raising money for a new venture. If you estimate that you will need, say, $10 million total to get your new enterprise to a point that it will be a suitable target for being acquired or doing an IPO, you'll do best if you think about whom you'll raise the *last* round of money from and what they'll need to convince them to invest, and then work backward to figure out the best sources for your initial seed round of funding. Nor is it very different from planning a successful product launch for, say, a new medical diagnostic. In those cases you think about how to gain the acceptance of the FDA, the major labs, and the biggest health insurers, and from there you work backward to fill in the other people you will need earlier in the process, just as Cytyc did.

Once you've identified the people you'll need, the task shifts to how to get their support. This is where the selling part comes in. But the kind of selling we're talking about is quite different from what we often see and experience. The difference can be summarized in one word: *empathy*. Here's what we mean.

Much of what people often call selling is really advertising; a mostly one-way broadcast, in verbal or printed form, intended to convince or coerce someone else to do something we want them to do, whether such actions are in their interests or not. Most people on the receiving end of such broadcasts hate the experience, and many people who are asked to do the transmitting also approach the whole ordeal with dread.

We think that a more effective, and pleasant, form of selling starts with a different goal; figuring out how we can achieve what we want *while* giving the other parties more of what they want—for real, not for show. And that's where empathy, the ability to understand and enter into another's feelings, comes into play. This doesn't mean identifying with the other people or becoming them or even liking them; it does mean *being able to perceive the world as they might*. That kind of empathetic knowledge gives better odds of structuring a deal that the other parties will find attractive to a greater or lesser extent, or identifying the warning signals of so little common ground that you'd be better off seeking support elsewhere.

So while our emphasis on empathetic selling may seem idealistic (and it is a nicer way of motoring through life than barraging people with endless pitches and one-way broadcasts), it's really a matter of practicality. The more you understand how another person models the world—not in a clinical way but in an empathetic way *from the other person's felt point of view*—the better you can predict how that person will react to matters of importance to you in the future. And the better you can predict how someone will react in the future, the faster and better you can determine how big of a shared agenda, if any, you can create with the people you want to recruit to your campaign.

A simple way of looking at this is to think about three broad categories of people: those with whom you have important and enduring overlaps, or your Core Allies; those with whom you can build temporary or situational overlaps that will be mutually beneficial, or The Possibles; and those with whom you have few motivations in common and who may even stand in opposition to your goals, or the Null-Setters.

## Category 1: Core Allies

Core Allies are the people with whom you share fundamental values and interests. They model how the world works pretty much as you do, and where they see things from another perspective, you understand the differences well enough to be able to anticipate what they would do in a variety of circumstances. You trust these people over a broad range of issues because you feel fairly comfortable predicting that their future actions will support your mutual goals.

Core Allies are crucial because these are the people you want to truly collaborate with, and they are the people you will usually call on first as you begin to build any campaign. Paul Revere and other Massachusetts revolutionaries were Core Allies. In a healthy family, you and your spouse, you and your parents, or you and your sibs and kids are all Core Allies for each other. You may not agree about everything with your Core Allies—there have even been known instances of Red Sox fans and Yankee fans who have been strong Core Allies for years except for issues related to the ball field—but you share enough fundamental values to trust each other on central bets in your lives.

Do you know who your Core Allies are and how to keep them involved in your campaign? It can be easy to confuse The Possibles with Core Allies, and therefore put too much trust in people who have less long-term overlap with your goals and interests. It's also easy to take the people who have been Core Allies in the past for granted; that can be a common problem in business, and also in marriages and families and friendships.

Your task, once you've identified your Core Allies, is to nurture and strengthen the fundamental bonds that unite you. In the language of the Square Dance of the Politicos, *Big foot up and little foot down, Grab your own and swing 'em around.*

## Category 2: The Possibles

The Possibles are the people whose desires and wants fit with yours on a situational basis—for a particular bet or set of bets—and there are a lot more of these people, usually by orders of magnitude, than there are Core Allies. You can model the likely fit of your interests with theirs on a case-by-case basis—that is, on this assignment or for that goal—but not necessarily on a fundamental or ongoing basis.

You don't collaborate with The Possibles on a long-term and trusted basis as much as you go along and work alongside them on particular projects or in particular situations. The further out you go on your who list, the more likely it is that you're looking at people who fall into The Possibles category for you. These are the swing voters, people whose support you have to earn on a case-by-case basis, just as want-to-be office holders have to do in a political campaign. Sometimes, people you work or play with and assume will be lifelong friends in fact fit in The Possibles category; they are great to pal around with when you are together, but there's not that much linking you together if one of you changes companies or moves to a new town or city.

Never ignore people in The Possibles category. Because there are so many of them, these swing voters can tip the balance for success or failure. And despite their numbers, they are not always obvious. In corporate settings, the swing voters for your campaigns can be your supervisors, bosses, board members, colleagues, or subordinates—all people who at first glance you might expect to fall in the Core Allies category. For General McClellan, the swing voters he may have worried about were the brass in Washington, which may be why he delayed action on the front in Antietam until he could gain their concurrence with his revised battle plans. For Howard, a fair number of the business people he approached for the Harvard Business School capital campaign also fell into this category.

Your key task with the people and organizations you see as possible situational allies is to expand the amount of overlap between your interests and theirs. You can do that best if you understand, empathically, what they care about and why. And, as a twist, you have to do this without alienating (or at least not irrevocably alienating) your Core Allies.

The beauty of this is that expanding the overlap with The Possibles is often fun, easy, and even not very costly, because frequently what the other people want is in your interests too. If you are trying to sell a house, figure out how to be a good client of the real estate agents and they will be able to do a better job for you (especially if you take the time beforehand to find good agents). If you are trying to get your venture funded, use the funders' concerns about how they will make money from backing you to understand your own business model better while still being true to the science or technology that inspired you.

In all these cases, it's the swing voters you're trying to reach, and your best shot for reaching them is to expand the area of overlap between your interests and theirs. Back to the calls at Square Dance of the Politicos: *Hold your partner, and your corner too, Now wave at the gal across from you.*

## Category 3: The Null-Setters

Null-Setters are the final group. These are people with whom you have little overlap or whose interests and goals are directly in opposition to yours. When you try to predict what they might do in future circumstances, you find yourself either at a loss or, worse, pretty sure that the other people will try to harm you in some way.

Many people, particularly those skilled in negotiation, believe that it is possible to find common ground with anyone, including the Null-

Setters, and therefore that doing so is a worthy goal. We do not sub-
scribe to this philosophy. The reason goes back to the idea of the 100
marbles. If the Null-Setters are people who could hurt us, then converting them at least to being willing to sit out the game may be worth
our investment of time and money. Otherwise, unless converting the
Null-Setters is essential to our goal, we'd rather use our time and
energy to build stronger bonds with our Core Allies and The Possibles. Besides, as far as we're concerned, life's too short to bother with
people we know are likely to try to hurt us, unless we absolutely have
to. Our theory for these kinds of cases is: when the lamb and the lion
lie down together, only the lamb need be afraid.

## AND CHECK THE VAPOR TRAIL

Most actions leave a mark—a footprint, or a vapor trail, or a leftover
clue. In presidential political campaigns in the United States, these vapor trails are becoming more and more evident, because television
coverage is more national, the Net is more ubiquitous, and electronic
databases are more extensive and easier to use, all providing increas-
ing numbers of opportunities for opponents to trip a candidate up
with past mistakes or contradictory positions.

In fact, for all of us, in our business lives and our personal ones,
the choices we make create vapor trails that others can eventually see
or find out about. Some of these are positive—an unexpected kind-
ness, ungrudging help, cheer, or optimism. Others are negative—a
lunge for the last little bit of everything, unfairness in negotiations,
distorted accounts of events, or attempts to sabotage or backstab.

Both kinds can have unbelievably long half-lives; sometimes the
smallest things come back to tip the balance for or against you decades later, invisibly to you, but with real effect. Thinking forward
can help you anticipate the kinds of vapor trails different approaches
might result in and therefore what your preferred approach should
be. And looking back at past vapor trails might help you anticipate

how willing various people are going to be to join your current campaign.

Do you know what vapor trails you have left in the past?

\* \* \* \*

Empathy is a hidden weapon of the smart gambler. The more you understand the world from the point of view of the people whose help you need, the better able you will be to structure situations in which they will want to use some of *their* marbles to help you in *your* campaigns. And the more you can align their interests with yours, the more you are making your own luck.

## MISS MISSISSIPPI, 1959

*Daisy Fay Harper is the heroine of Fannie Flagg's wonderful novel,* Daisy Fay and the Miracle Man. *If PowerPoint had been around in 1959 during Daisy Fay's campaign to win the Miss Mississippi pageant, this would have been the slide her friends would have put together to help her get the people she would need on her side—the judges:*

---

### OBJECTIVE: Make Sure the Judges Like You

*How to do it: Trick the judges*

| **If they ask you** | **You must say (even if you don't believe it)** |
|---|---|
| • *Who you admire most in the world* | • *Your mother or Joan Crawford (either one is surefire)* |
| • *What you want out of life* | • *To be a good American and a Christian mother* |
| • *What your hobbies are* | • *Teaching Sunday School and working with poor children* |

*Remember, whatever you do,* DON'T TELL THE TRUTH!
*Use the answers above!*

*Source: Our survey of questions to past Miss Mississippi contestants, and the answers given by the winners.*

---

*Daisy Fay succeeded in her campaign and won the contest. If you were Aesop, transported to the twenty-first century, and you knew how Daisy Fay had prepared for this competition, what moral would you draw from this story, and why?*

# The Gambler's Dozen, Step 5

# IMPLICIT STRATEGY:
## Find the Current Bets

# Happily Ever After

ALL things considered, when Scheherazade agreed to marry King Shahryar, the odds didn't look very good that she'd be queen for more than a day.

That's because King S, in consequence of having been deceived by a former wife, had since instituted a policy of marrying every evening, and having his new queen executed the following morning. As one might imagine, the king's practice of a wedding every night and an execution every morning was depleting his kingdom's stock of marriageable maidens, had spread unimaginable fear and grief throughout the land, and had certainly reduced the king's chances to produce an heir to his throne.

Scheherazade was very beautiful and very smart, and determined too, and her goal was to end the killings and keep her own life in the process. So late on her marriage night, and before the king fell asleep, Scheherazade began to tell a story for the king's pleasure, a fantastic tale of sorcerers and genies and pirates and sailors and legendary places. And just as the sun began to rise, and the executioner made ready, Scheherazade got to the most exciting part of her story—and the king therefore delayed her execution for twenty-four hours, so he could hear what happened next. And the next night, the same thing happened, and the night after that as well, and so on for the next 1,001 nights. And by the last of those nights, Scheherazade had borne the king three sons, and he had fallen in love with her, and then she and he did in fact live happily ever after.

If you grew up hearing the stories of Aladdin's Lamp, Ali Baba

and the Forty Thieves, or Sinbad the Sailor, you know why
Scheherazade's stories, as recounted in the fourteenth-century Arabic
classic *The Book of One Thousand and One Nights*, kept King
Shahryar on pins and needles, eagerly awaiting the next installment.

In the game of marital poker, Scheherazade had poor cards and
not many chips. But she placed her bets based on a clear understanding of the rules and odds that would govern their outcomes, which is
a more reliable asset than magic, even in fairy tales.

# 5. Implicit Strategy: How Much Magic Will My Current Bets Require?

IT'S amazing how often people think they are placing bets that will get them to one kind of outcome, when the real bets they are placing, or what we think of as their "implicit strategy," are leading them someplace else entirely, or will require a hefty dose of magic to get anywhere close to a satisfactory outcome. Scheherazade was not one of those people, because she understood the real nature of the bets she was placing and had the skills and discipline to manage them well, but millions of the rest of us often are.

A great example is the diet industry. In the United States alone, sales of weight-loss products tipped the scales at over $40 billion in 2000, with growth of about 6 percent per year. Despite all these products, Americans are still getting fatter and fatter, and Europeans are too; current numbers suggest that approximately two in every three Americans are now overweight, as are about one in two Europeans. And, over any five-year period, 95 percent of people who have lost weight can expect to regain what they lost, often with interest. With so many people investing so much in weight-loss bets, how come there are so few winners (except, of course, for the companies that sell the over $40 billion worth of diet stuff to the dieters)?

We think the answer, for most people, goes back to the fifth skill of Predictive Intelligence, and the basis for this step in the Gambler's Dozen: seeing and assessing your *real* bets, rather than the bets you think you are taking or that you describe to others as your current or intended bets. This is an OO—Orient and Organize—skill, and it requires you to understand the true nature of the current bets you are placing, and the degree to which skill and discipline, versus magic and dumb luck, will determine your ability to convert these bets into sustainable wins.

One way to test how and why an understanding of implicit strategy can explain the long-term failure of many weight-loss bets is to take a quick look at your own or your friends' experiences in the battle of the bulge.

When Eileen did this, she immediately saw the obvious: her weight was a direct consequence of what she was currently eating. Even worse, some of what she was currently eating she didn't really care about. Despite what she had been telling herself and others, her implicit strategy—as measured by what she *did* rather than what she said—had been to maintain her current size.

Seeing your real strategy can be discomforting. It also gives you the opportunity to see how fast you can revamp your implicit strategy to get the outcomes you desire. Eileen's experiment for this was to skip the idea of a diet entirely, and instead start at the end and go directly to a postdiet regimen she thought she could maintain long-term. She did this by cutting out the stuff she was currently eating and didn't care about—a bread roll some days at lunch, an extra glass of wine other nights at dinner, the occasional second cookie at meetings—and then seeing what her new weight would be. That was it— which, for her, turned out to be reasonably effective, painless, and easy.

Of course, this isn't rocket science, and it isn't magic. The math of caloric inputs and outputs dictates that most people, if they cut out a net 75 to 150 calories a day, as Eileen did, will lose about five or ten pounds over the course of a year, and will keep the pounds off if they don't add these calories back. But many people don't make such modest cuts in the way they eat or additions to the way they exercise. Instead, they opt for diets that provide good odds for quick and sometimes dramatic temporary victories but pretty reliably will not give them sustainable wins, no matter how much money they invest in the attempts or what they tell themselves or others about their new diets.

There's a generalizable lesson here, and it extends far beyond fairy tales and the diet industry. Whether your objective is related to your company's future, or your marriage, or your health, or the motivation of your workforce, you need to be conscious of your implicit strategy—the nature of the bets you are actually placing—and to be able to assess where those bets are likely to lead versus where you really want to go.

Seeing and assessing the implicit strategy being followed is the purpose of this step. Our approach starts with identifying the currency of the bets—the kind of marbles you will be investing. This makes it easier for us to cut through the words and see the wagers. Then we assess whether these bets, pursued with skill and discipline, have a reasonable shot of delivering the desired results, or whether there's such a sizable gap that a big dose of magic and dumb luck will be required as well. If the answer is more magic than skill, we look at the simplest remedies of all—we either change our bets to match our goals, or we change our goals to match our bets so we don't require magic or an excess of good fortune to succeed.

## FOLLOW THE CURRENCY TO DECIPHER THE CURRENT BETS

Every bet has its currency, the type of assets or marbles you place at risk in hopes of getting the future return you desire. For poker, the bets are denominated in chips, backed by cash. For strategy for companies and nonprofits, the critical resource usually is also cash, as it is for personal investing. For relationships—friendships, marriages, family—often the asset that matters most is time and attention (real attention, not going to a kid's soccer game and then yakking on a cell phone as the play proceeds). For weight management for most people, it's calories in versus calories out, plus ongoing attention to these inputs and outputs. And for Scheherazade, it was her storehouse of fabulous stories and her ability to tell these tales in a tantalizing way.

Following the currency of the bet reveals the essence of any implicit strategy. In the corporate world, this means following the money, and it saves a ton of time. Here's how we do it: First we look at the business plans, corporate strategy plans, accompanying Power-Point presentations, and all the statements—you know, the mission statement, the vision statement, the principles and values statement, and whatever. We skim all these documents so we understand what the people in the company say to themselves about their strategies and the outcomes they wish to achieve. Then we look at the budgets for both capital investments and operating expenses and follow where the money is coming from and where it is going. You'd be surprised, in the spirit of a column of figures is worth a thousand words, at how much a few numbers can tell you.

Take the case of Mercury Power, in New Zealand. Mercury was set up in 1992 as a semiprivatized company, taking over the job of supplying electricity from the government, and serving Auckland, New Zealand's commercial center and largest city. The company promptly proclaimed itself as the reliable, "no-worries power" company.

But a look at the books shows Mercury's actual bets had way less to do with reliable power delivery than it did with fast growth of its revenue and asset base, and an eventual IPO of a portion of its shares. First the company raised its rates to its Auckland customers and started laying off employees, including some of the maintenance staff who tended to Mercury's four forty-year-old underground power cables that supplied all the electricity to Auckland's central business district. Then the company began to use the cash it was amassing to mount hostile takeover attempts, especially of archenemy Utilicorp for control of another New Zealand company, Power New Zealand.

Unfortunately, and as Mercury management had previously been informed, two of the power cables were at imminent risk of total malfunction. This was particularly worrisome because failure of any one of the four cables would quickly trigger cascading failures of all of the remaining ones.

And that's in fact exactly what did happen in the heat of Auckland's summer in 1998, leading to a two-month total blackout of

Auckland's central commercial area, and we do mean total—no electricity, no computers, no air-conditioning, no elevators, no nothing for over two months, except for what nasty and stinky temporary diesel generators, hastily placed on sidewalks throughout the city and on a ship anchored in the harbor, could produce. One might say that rather than bringing "no-worries power" to its customers, Mercury created massive "no-power worries."

Mercury management offered many explanations. First they ascribed the prolonged blackout to "a freakish series of events," then to the El Niño weather pattern, and later to damage from traffic vibration and land movement. But the truth is in the numbers: Mercury talked about service but bet on expansion and an eventual IPO—and enough luck that the cables wouldn't give out until they had the time and interest in fixing them, perhaps after the share float. One has to wonder, did the execs at Mercury not understand the real nature of the bets they were placing? Or did they have a clear idea of the bets but not of how much good fortune they would need to achieve anything close to a successful outcome?

Mercury is not alone in paying too little attention to understanding their implicit strategies based on the real bets they are placing. Lots of companies talk about people being their most important asset when a look at the books shows relatively poor compensation and benefits to all but the top few execs, and little investment in benefits and training. Other companies talk about innovation when their numbers show less than industry-average investments in R&D, with more of the funds going into development and enhancements of existing products than into research and invention of new products.

If you know the currency of the bets, with a little digging you can see the bets themselves. Then you are in position to assess whether converting these bets into the results you desire will be a matter primarily of skill—or one of chance.

# MIND THE GAP TO ASSESS
# THE MAGIC QUOTIENT

Once you see your real bets, you may also see a gap between the chips and skills you have to invest and the goals to which you aspire.

The question then is, if you see a gap, is it a gap that only magic or very good fortune can bridge? Then, like Cinderella or Mercury Power or most dieters, your real bet is that chance and dumb luck will allow you to achieve and hold onto what you desire and perhaps think you deserve.

Or do you see a gap that, while big, is one that you will be able to bridge with a series of feasible bets even though you can't outline all these bets in detail right now? That's more akin to what Collins and Porras, the authors of *Built to Last*, call a BHAG, Big Hairy Audacious Goal. Then you also believe—like Scheherazade or Paul Revere and his fellow revolutionaries—that you will be able to keep leveraging your assets into progressively better positions until you reach your goal.

Your answer to these questions will tell you whether you need to chuck or massively revise your current bets because they are highly unlikely to get you where you want to go, or whether you can use them as a reasonable first draft of how to up your odds of achieving what you wish to achieve.

This isn't to say that all big gaps are bad; yawning gaps seem to be the rule rather than the exception in the business plans of new enterprises. And actually, we're quite fond of ham-and-eggs strategies—as in if I had ham, I could have ham and eggs, if I had eggs—as long as we understand what we really have (like a skillet, for example) and what we need, so we can begin to use all our skills and chips to beg, borrow, or buy (at a discount) the eggs. That's what Bill Gates did in 1980 as he was convincing IBM about Microsoft's ability to deliver an operating system for the new personal computer IBM was then developing, and later on what Michael Dell did too, when he was in his dorm room figuring out a cheaper way to assemble and sell laptops.

It's also true that in some cases where the gap is big, sometimes the better path is simply to change your goals and hold onto your bets. If you think about people (other than yourself, of course) as interchangeable widgets, maybe it's better to invest your betting chips into standardizing tasks and training, so you keep operating without a hitch even with a revolving door of people. If you'd like to be a leading drug discovery company but can't stand the risk and the failure rates, maybe it's better to pick up underutilized pharma assets and leverage your sales and manufacturing skills as King Pharmaceutical did in its early years.

What's not so great is to fall into the Powerball trap and stick with a bet with terrible odds.

Powerball Lottos in the United States require players to pick five numbers between 1 and 53 plus one additional number between 1 and 42 for the Powerball, and they carry odds of hitting the jackpot of just a bit over 1 in 120,000,000. Now say the jackpot for this week's Powerball lottery is $256,000,000. If you take your life savings, or take a $100,000 loan out on the equity of your house, and buy up 100,000 tickets at a dollar apiece, you will bring your odds down a 100,000-fold and your new odds will be—1 in 1,200. Odds of 1 in 1,200 stink, yet plenty of people and businesses invest in bets that don't have much better chances of success, hoping against hope that somehow their ticket will be the lucky one.

How about your implicit strategy? When you look at the chips you have to invest, the cards you hold, and the rules and odds that will govern the outcomes on your bets, do you think that, with enough discipline and perhaps a little luck, you can get where you want to go? Or do you have an implicit strategy that's filled with lots of details, until you get to that part in the middle that requires a miracle or two to suddenly occur? Magic thinking in business (and life) decisions may reduce anxiety—and maybe that's why it appears in so many business plans—but it's a poor way to bet. If the odds are slim that your current set of bets will get you where you want to go unless a major miracle intervenes, you might want to reconsider whether more bets in the same vein are just bringing totally atrocious odds down to new odds that are merely horrendous.

\*    \*    \*    \*

Magic thinking is widespread in all kinds of bets—corporate bets, career bets, and life bets. Once you spot it in your bets, you have the power to change your destiny by either changing your bets to ones with better odds of achieving your goals—or changing your goals to fit your actual bets.

On the other hand, if you spot a habit of magic thinking in the executives of a company you are thinking of investing in or partnering with—or a person you think you want to spend a significant portion of your life with (unless that person is a toddler)—we have only one piece of advice: if you can't get those people to revise their approach, run in the opposite direction as fast as you can.

## PEANUT BUTTER AND JELLY

*First day on the latest job site and Jack, Mickey, and Bob are on lunch break, sitting on a girder on what will be the thirty-eighth floor of a new skyscraper. Jack unpacks his lunch pail, hoists out a big baguette, takes a bite, and says, "Ham and cheese with hot mustard! Excellent!" Mickey unpacks his lunch pail, pulls out some cold barbeque chicken, and says, as he chomps into one of the drumsticks, "Great, chicken, my favorite!" Then Bob opens his lunch pail, unwraps the paper, and reveals a peanut butter and jelly sandwich. On white bread. And mutters, "Peanut butter and jelly! I hate peanut butter and jelly!"*

*On Tuesday, lunch break, same girder, Jack unpacks his lunch pail and brings forth a Thermos of hot chili and a couple of slabs of corn bread. He smacks his lips and chows down. Mickey opens his lunch pail and exclaims with pleasure as he unwraps a big Italian sub. And then Bob opens his pail, and reveals . . . a peanut butter and jelly sandwich on white bread. And he swears under his breath, "Damn peanut butter and jelly! I hate peanut butter and jelly!"*

*On Wednesday, Jack unpacks his lunch and finds a tuna sub, just the way he likes it, and three chocolate chip cookies. Mickey discovers that he has his absolute favorite—a turkey, ham, and cheese sandwich, plus a big bag of chips. And then Bob unpacks his pail, and discovers . . . a peanut butter and jelly sandwich on white bread. And he swears a blue streak about how much he hates frigging peanut butter and jelly.*

*So Jack turns to him, and says, "Dude, if you hate peanut butter and jelly that much, why don't you ask your wife to pack you something else?"*

*To which Bob responds, "Wife? What wife? I make my lunch myself."*

*What should Bob pack in his lunch pail on Thursday? Why?*

# The Gambler's Dozen, Step 6

# PLAN B:
# Create a Real Alternative

# Tom Hoving Does Tut

ALL fields seem to have markets for their own insider gossip, and as far as we can tell the art world is no exception.

One person who created plenty of buzz in the 1970s was Thomas Hoving, then director of the Metropolitan Museum of Art in New York and son of the chairman of Tiffany's. At the Met, Hoving was a master impresario, and looked and acted the part: cosmopolitan and erudite with a PhD in art history, tall and elegant in aspect, comfortable in a tux.

As director, Hoving dreamed big and acted bigger. He secured the blockbuster exhibit "The Treasures of Tutankamen," the inspiration for the Steve Martin classic "King Tut" (available at www.steve martin.com). He dismantled the entire Temple of Dendur from its original location in Egypt and had it reassembled, stone by stone, at the museum. And he expanded the footprint of the Met into Central Park.

It was the expansion in the park that sparked one of the hot stories that made the rounds in the art community. It went like this: When Hoving wanted to expand into the park, he had his best team put together their best ideas and these became the baseline plan. Then he hired the best law firm in New York to write the brief *against* that plan. He followed this by hiring the *second-best* law firm in New York to create a Plan B that could withstand the arguments developed by the first firm. Only then did he unveil the Met's goal of expanding into the park, using of course his Plan B, which had replaced the original plan.

Now his opponents were stymied because they simply didn't have enough time to come up with a counterpunch. Since Hoving had already come up with his "best" plan—the original one—and then made it better by building in a defense to likely objections—his Plan B—the opponents couldn't counterattack in time.

This is a wonderful story with one problem, which Eileen discovered when she chatted with Hoving before introducing him to an audience of very somber and serious MBAs: it isn't true. Hoving did tell Eileen the real story, which she promptly forgot, because she likes this one better.

Two good things came out of this discussion, though. First, Eileen discovered that a good parable needn't be literally true to communicate a true lesson, in this case, the power of Plan Bs. And second, she got Hoving to sing and dance Martin's King Tut routine for the audience before giving his speech.

# 6. Plan B: What's the Best I Could Do if My Current Plan Gets Blocked?

"HAVE you thought about what you are going to do if . . . ?" is the question that underlies the creation of any good Plan B, the sixth skill of Predictive Intelligence and the focus of this step of the Gambler's Dozen. It's the question you answer intuitively if you bring a fat book you've been meaning to read and a list of alternate flights when you go to the airport. It's also the question venture capitalists answer explicitly when they use their estimate of the number of "shots on goal" for a prospective portfolio company as a criterion for investment. And it's the question answered not only in the apocryphal parable of Thomas Hoving and the Metropolitan Museum of Art, but also in the true story of Billy Beane and the Oakland A's baseball team.

If you've taken a look at Michael Lewis's *Moneyball*, you know the tale of how Beane joined the front office of the Oakland A's in 1993, and became increasingly interested in how to use baseball statistics to refine the key bets of who to recruit and how to play them. This was not a terribly popular thing to do at the time because much of what the statistics reveal about factors that correlate with success runs counter to the conventional wisdom of the game.

In 1993, the statistics said the more walks a player draws, the bigger a contributor he would be to an effective baseball offense. Baseball wisdom in 1993 said that walks-per-player data were at best irrelevant and at worst a red flag about the player. Beane figured that if the statistics were right and if they also went against conventional wisdom, the few managers who believed the statistics would be able to pick up gems at bargain-basement prices while the other teams would overpay for kids who fit the traditional metrics. But as is often the case in the battle of facts against gut feelings, the A's ignored Beane and continued with their existing betting strategy, high payroll and all.

Still, Beane persevered and he and others in the A's organization kept working on an alternate set of bets based on the factors for success the stats indicated. This obsession ultimately turned out to be very important for the A's. Not in 1993 when Walter Haas owned the A's, because Haas's goal was to win at any cost. But in 1995 after Haas died, because then the team was sold to new owners who didn't like the "at any cost" part of the Haas philosophy and who cranked the money tap way back.

Almost overnight, the Oakland A's went from having one of the highest payrolls in the league to having one of the lowest. Almost as quickly, Beane's Plan B for the team began to look pretty good. And so, over time, have the results. In 1991, under Haas, the A's had the highest payroll in all of baseball. In 2002, under the new owners, the payroll for the A's was one of the two lowest in baseball and, at $40 million, was *less than a third* of that of the New York Yankees, who spent $126 million on its players. Yet with 103 wins, the A's still tied the Yanks for the most wins in the majors that year and they clinched the AL West championship. Figuring out a good Plan B—*before* you need it—can be invaluable, in business as in baseball.

Do you have a Plan B in mind now? Developing and testing a Plan B that's solid enough that you could rely on it if you had to is the skill this step is based on. This is the last of the OO—Orient and Organize—skills that make up the OOPA! process, and its focus is on organizing a solid Plan B, before you find yourself in circumstances that force you to reinvent your bets on the fly.

Our approach to testing our own Plan Bs is first to do a thought experiment on our current Plan B to see if we have dared to think broadly and even radically enough—or just looked at minor variations on our existing baseline plan or, alternately, created a draconian Plan B that can be immediately rejected. Then, if we pass the dare test, we go on the hunt for the silver linings of our Plan B, looking for new benefits or new ways to mitigate risks that can't be gained by the existing plan. We don't always find these silver linings, but when we do, we either incorporate them into our base plan or, like Hoving and Beane, move directly to use the Plan B as our new base plan.

## TO DARE OR NOT TO DARE, ESPECIALLY WHERE ELEPHANTS LURK

Two things get in the way of strong Plan Bs, we find. One is speed-boat wakes. The other is elephants.

Speedboat wakes occur when you're going pretty fast, or just fast enough, that in your haste you've neglected to figure out a Plan B at all, or have done a sloppy job of it so that you're looking only at small variations from your existing plan, or haven't really aimed at creating a great Plan B.

We don't worry much about poor Plan Bs due to lack of attention while speeding along on the baseline plan, because these kinds of problems are easy to fix *if* you choose to fix them. In these cases, you can slow down just long enough to ask yourself the concrete what-if questions that can get you started on a better Plan B. These are the basic questions we started this chapter with: what if a community group challenges your museum's plans for expansion, what if your flight gets canceled, what if your lead product fails its final tests, what if new owners cut the amount of money you can spend in the college draft for players? Once you have an idea of what you would want to be able to do in these what-if situations, you have the raw materials for a better Plan B.

And then there are the elephants. More specifically, elephants who reside in living rooms.

The classic elephant-in-the-living-room situation looks like this: there's a very big problem; the problem is growing with increasingly bad consequences; and no one wants to shoot the elephant. Take the very large industrial company that was losing share in several of its largest divisions that historically had been the leaders in their respective markets. Corporate management had decided that this problem was due to a lack of marketing expertise, and therefore invested heavily in a big companywide marketing initiative and targeted one of the divisions that was suffering from most worrisome share losses to be the first candidate for the new marketing-excellence program. A team of consultants and corporate officers was then dispatched to the division.

But here was the real problem, discovered in *one day* of interviews of the midlevel people in the organization: The division made small but very important widgets that went into very big machines produced by the division's customers. The big machines were made on assembly lines that required the widgets to go in before the next steps of the manufacturing process could be started, and when the widgets weren't delivered on time, the entire production line had to be stopped, at enormous cost to the customers. The division was missing its delivery dates often, even after original delivery dates had been confirmed repeatedly. Competitors, who didn't have anywhere close to the scale and financial strength of the division, were gaining sales and building their reputations simply by delivering the products they said they would deliver on the days they said they would deliver them.

A look at the manufacturing configuration of the big company pinpointed the elephant—nine factories, each producing some but not all of the components that went into the widgets, with factory managers who had no direct accountability to the heads of the product divisions for either shipping the correct products or delivering them on time. The resulting lost revenues to the company were estimated to be in the hundreds of millions of dollars.

The implicit strategy for this company was to talk service, add some bells and whistles to its marketing programs, and, most importantly, make no material changes to the way manufacturing was measured and managed. The Plan B proposed by the outsiders was to consolidate production for the division's products into fewer, or even into one, manufacturing facility, and make the factory managers accountable for on-time delivery to the customers.

It would be difficult to overstate the degree of active antipathy that greeted this Plan B, from top managers at both the division and the corporate levels. Delivery wasn't a problem, they said, despite the company's own reports that showed that it was. The manufacturing problem had been "solved" eighteen months ago, resulting in the current configuration of factories and reporting relationships, and it would be politically unwise and personally unpleasant to revisit the issue. Okay, perhaps there was a problem, and even though the numbers indicated that the situation was spiraling downward, maybe the worst was over. And, anyway, wouldn't the customers love us again if we marketed better? The good news in this sorry mess is that about six months later corporate management decided to shoot the elephant and reorganize the manufacturing function so that the customers' core needs could be met adequately and reliably.

All sorts of organizations face all sorts of elephants—poor acquisitions that aren't working, new hires or promotions who are creating more problems than they are solving, pet projects that are soaking up time and resources with little promise of anything other than marginal returns at best. At a more personal level, alcoholics and their families and friends face similar issues. So do victims of domestic violence, people in bad relationships or in bad job situations, and sometimes even individuals who have always been healthy but are suddenly confronting serious illnesses. In all these cases, the people resisting even considering a real Plan B tend to share two characteristics: they prefer to believe that the problem, if they see it at all, is surely going to be better tomorrow; and they feel that acknowledging that the problem exists would be deeply humiliating.

Of course, in most of these cases, as in the story of the big company that was losing share, the situation is not getting better and most everyone close to the organization or the person already knows about the problem. As the old joke that little kids like to tell: How do you know if there's an elephant in bed with you? You can smell the peanuts on his breath.

If you're smelling the peanuts, dare to create a real Plan B, a plan that allows you to address the elephant and the problems it is creating directly. That's one of the single most important ways you can up the odds and make your own luck.

## ON THE HUNT FOR SILVER LININGS

Creating strong Plan Bs isn't fun. We both hate it. One reason we hate it is that we've already invested effort in creating our existing plan and, like many people, we tend to love our current plans or at least we get to feeling very comfortable with them, and in any case we want to just go off and do what we said we wanted to do. Still, we try to discipline ourselves to figure out the best we could do if our planned set of bets gets blocked.

For one thing, we know that our planned set of bets could, in fact, get blocked and we want to be able to respond well if that happens. And for another, we like the silver linings we often find in our Plan Bs in the form of additional upsides, or better ways to mitigate risks, or both. Then we have four options: replace our existing plan with Plan B; revise our existing plan with selected pieces from our Plan B; stick with the existing plan but prepare a contingency plan based on our Plan B; or work like hell because there's no option but to make the planned set of bets succeed.

Replacing the current plan happens remarkably frequently—when you have the discipline to really try to create the best Plan B you can. In these cases, and when the aggregate silver linings are sufficient, you may want to chuck the existing plan and go with Plan B pretty much in its entirety. That's the point of the apocryphal Hoving parable, and that's what any person or company does when they take on an elephant that has been messing up their living room.

Most of the rest of the time, the effort to create a great Plan B will give you ideas for improving the existing plan and building solid contingency plans. That's what Billy Beane and others in the A's organization did from 1993 to 1995, and that's what we do when we bring extra reading material and ideas for alternate travel arrangements when we go to the airport.

And finally there are those situations where, hard as you might try, you can find no Plan B that is even remotely acceptable. These situations are reasonably rare in our experience, but they do occur. If you find yourself in such a spot, and you know that whatever you do the results will be critically important to your future, you are in a do-or-die situation. Then your only intelligent option is to check that you are devoting all the resources—time, energy, attention, money—that your Plan A requires.

Some people use the possibly apocryphal story of Vikings burning their ships on the shore as the best model for how to build commitment to a strategy, or the true story of Spanish explorer Hernando Cortes burning his ships in 1519 in Mexico for the same reason; if you have no other alternatives, you will fight all the harder to prevail (and your crew won't see mutiny as a viable Plan B). Frankly, though, we can think of better things to do with our adrenaline—plus, using our brains to up our odds makes more sense to us than the equivalent of burning our ships, unless we have no other viable alternative.

*   *   *   *

Time is one of your biggest enemies when events unfold differently from what you had planned or hoped. Having a Plan B in mind, even a very rough Plan B, puts you in position to respond well and in the time available. Other people may watch the way you react and adjust to the new circumstances and think that you are very lucky, but you will know that you have made your own luck by having thought through your Plan B—before you needed it.

## DEAL MAKING IN THE BOARDROOM

*The investment banker who tells this story swears that it is true. Since he was there and we weren't, we have no reason to not believe him.*

*It seems that the banker was representing the seller's side in a transaction, and had gone to the headquarters of the company that wished to buy the assets to finalize the deal terms. When the banker named the price required for the prospective buyer to pick up the assets, the management team on the buy side all looked at each other, and then the senior-most person looked at the banker and said, "Would you excuse us for a moment, please?"*

*"Certainly," said the banker.*

*When the group came back, the leader of the acquiring company said, "We've had a prayer, and the Lord says the price is too high."*

*Without missing a beat, the banker said, "Go back and tell the Lord He just lost you the deal."*

*The leader looked at the banker and said, "Would you excuse us again, please?"*

*Two minutes later the group came back and the leader said, "The Lord said the deal is alright after all."*


*If you were a professor evaluating the quality of Plan B thinking done by the management team of the company that wanted to buy the assets that the banker was selling, what grade would you give and why?*

# The
# Predict and Act!
# Steps

The Gambler's Dozen, Step 7

# PREDICTION MAPS:
## Chart the Future Choice Points

## TEEN HAIKU

Buff teen gets tattooed.

Does she think gravity will

Never affect her?

# 7. Prediction Maps: What's the Future Space I'm Betting Into?

THE thing about betting is, it helps to think about the predictions you're making about key factors outside your control *before* you place your wager. That's the seventh skill of the Gambler's Dozen and it focuses on disciplined forecasting of the factors that will have the biggest impacts on future outcomes. This is a PA!—Predict and Act!—skill, and it's the foundation for the remaining steps in the OOPA! process.

We suspect that the buff dudes and dudettes of our haiku rarely think about such things and therefore pay little attention to how factors like gravity, for example, or changing tastes, or new loves, might affect their satisfaction years from now with the tattoos they love today. How many of us, at age fifteen, were able to imagine ever reaching age fifty-five, much less age fifty-five with a fifty-five–year-old body? And then would have been able to picture our age-progressed bodies with age-progressed tattoos—a pudgy and not very scary skull-and-bones perhaps, or a sad and sagging butterfly, or worst of all, the name of a former flame now long gone—any or all located on a strategic body part?

Companies often encounter a related problem when they analyze current industry structures with the aim of crafting changes they anticipate will turn the tables to their own advantage. The problem comes when, like the Tattooed Teen, they forget to figure in the future impacts of other elements of their competitive environments on the outcomes they wish to achieve. One company sees a need—say, broadband access to the Internet—and expands like crazy to fill the emerging demand. And so, unfortunately for that company, do a slew of others until, and usually very quickly, a glut of newly minted capacity kills industry profitability and pushes many of the once optimistic entrants into early graves.

And then there is the example of John Boyd.

\* \* \* \*

Col. John Boyd, USAF, was sent to Korea as a young fighter pilot in 1953. Being a fighter pilot, Boyd knew that battle landscapes change fast; the world in which a bet is planned is a different place than the world in which the bet is executed, and the world in which that bet then plays out will be different still. He also realized that, in his line of work at least, being able to decipher the emerging pattern faster and more accurately than the other guy was literally the difference between hitting a target or being hit.

In Boyd's Korea, the daily life-and-death target game of "hit or be hit" pitted American F-86s against Soviet MiG-15s. Back in Washington, Pentagon officials had already decided that the Soviet planes were far superior to the American ones because the MiGs were faster and could fly higher. That conclusion had led to a mad dash to develop a new U.S. fighter jet that could out-MiG the MiGs. Boyd wasn't so sure this was smart and, to the displeasure of more than a few of his higher-ups, said so. For one thing, he had flown F-86s in battle against the MiGs and was convinced, based on this experience, that the F-86 was the better plane. For another, he thought the kill ratio—about 14 to 1 in favor of the F-86—was a telling piece of evidence.

So Boyd asked some simple questions: What if the MiG's apparent advantages weren't the deciding factors in air battles? What if, instead, the F-86 had advantages that weren't appreciated on the ground in Washington but were making all the difference in the skies above Korea?

Which is exactly what Boyd decided was the case. The F-86, Boyd came to believe, had two essential advantages over the MiG-15: visibility and agility. The visibility advantage came from the F-86's transparent bubble cockpit canopy, which gave its pilots a broader and clearer field of vision. As a result, an F-86 pilot could see more of what was going on around him faster and therefore was better able to forecast future positions in an evolving battle. The agility advantage came from both the F-86's "flying tail" design (which gave it more maneuverability at high altitudes) and its hydraulic flight controls (which gave it more maneuverability at high speeds), providing the F-86s pilots with a wider and better range of options in many battle situations.

Boyd then articulated explicitly what people with high PIs, including great military strategists, have known intuitively all along: faster visibility and greater agility trump brute power. The faster you can get a good fix on the emerging patterns around you—those evolving external factors that will largely define what we think of as the "future space"—the better able you will be to see how to shed risk and up the odds of gaining your objectives. And the more agile you are, the better able you will be to make your own luck by capitalizing on these insights fast, when the opportunities are available.

As for the military, Boyd's views shook up a number of areas. Fighter-pilot education was one, and his training techniques are still in use today around the world. Military strategy is another. And that dream of a muscle plane that could out-MiG the MiGs? Over the stiff objections of some in the Pentagon, Boyd led a revolution that resulted in the next generation of fighter jets—the F-15, the F-16 especially, and the F-18—which leveraged the advantages of faster visibility and greater agility rather than going for more muscle mass.

Many people, including some tattooed teens and lots of people who act impulsively, are sloppy forecasters. To the extent they think at all about the predictions they are making, they think primarily about the immediate outcomes they desire. Their predictions are limited because their fields of vision are limited; they focus on only a few factors and only over very short time spans, and they often end up unhappy with the long-term consequences of their bets. Inadvertently, their risk/return profiles tend to be heavy on the risk and light on the returns.

Other people, like John Boyd, are disciplined forecasters. They make predictions about the future space *before* they make predictions about the outcomes of their bets, and they go fast by looking for emerging patterns rather than complete pictures. They end up in the right places more often than other people because they see where the right places are likely to be faster, and they are then willing to act on the emerging patterns they see.

* * * *

The previous six steps of the Gambler's Dozen have focused primarily on the orienting and organizing parts of OOPA!—figuring out goals, understanding implicit strategies, and making fast adjustments. With this step, we move more directly into the predicting and acting parts, working out the potential options and choosing which to pursue. We use Prediction Maps as a supporting tool for the rest of the PA! steps, and we use this chapter to show what these maps are and how we construct them.

The approach we've built into our Prediction Maps varies from standard business thinking in two ways. First, we believe that smart bettors reject the notion that higher returns always entail higher risk. For this reason we've structured our maps specifically to highlight opportunities for breaking this link to our advantage. And second, as always, we want to go fast. For this reason we've designed a process for drafting these maps that can be done very quickly and still provide the information we need to structure better bets.

## MAPPING THE FUTURE FOR MORE PAYOFF AND LESS RISK

How you frame an issue determines what you will see. We don't like the ideas that risk and return are a matched set and therefore that if you want more return, you have to take on more risk. And, back to

the principle of the 100 marbles, we also know that we have finite resources, both for figuring out the best bets to take and for investing in
the bets themselves. So when we map the future, we especially look
for opportunities to get more of what will help us with less uncertainty about the outcomes we will achieve. The format we have chosen for this search is a simple two-by-two matrix, which we use as a
rough-and-ready Prediction Map.

To construct this map we focus on future impacts of factors outside our direct control—gravity as one factor in the instance of the
buff teen, or the moves of competitors or government regulators as
common corporate examples. Then we sort these factors in two ways.
The first sort is by degree of impact each factor could have on the potential future payoffs (or, in the case of negative impacts, potential future losses) of our bets. This sort by degree of impact becomes the
vertical axis of our map. The second sort is by degree of uncertainty
and therefore the risk that the kind of impact we are forecasting resolves differently from what we expected. This sort by degree of uncertainty becomes the horizontal axis.

Here's a little more detail on each of these dimensions and a picture of the map.

The "Impact" dimension, the one on the vertical axis, helps us to
understand the range of potential returns on our bets because it
shows our estimates of the *relative impact the factor could have on
our future payoffs, including both potential gains and losses.* If you
work in a start-up pharmaceutical company and your lead compound is going through the FDA approval process, you know that
what the FDA says will be one of the ultrahigh-impact factors for
you and your company. A thumbs-up from the FDA, and you could
wake up rich; a thumbs-down, and you could see much of your enterprise value evaporating—as holders of stock in ImClone Systems,
Sam Waksal and Martha Stewart among them, discovered after the
FDA's December 2001 negative ruling on ImClone's lead cancer
drug, Erbitux.

The "Uncertainty" dimension, the one on the horizontal axis, gives us a way to estimate *the risk of betting based on the wrong side of a prediction, which occurs when you think a factor will move in one direction and then it moves in some other way.* Demographic trends, such as the graying of the populations of first-world countries, are relatively certain factors, which is good news for companies that sell ergonomic products, hair dyes, and hearing aids. Future oil prices tend to be at the other end of the spectrum because there is more variability, and therefore uncertainty, about which way the prices might go. Companies that invested in alternative energy plays over the past three decades on the expectation that oil prices would stay high know a lot about this risk, and have the battle scars (and the depleted bank accounts) to show for it.

Putting these two dimensions together gives this Prediction Map:

## Gambler's Dozen Prediction Map

| Relative Impact | | |
|---|---|---|
| **High** | Wallpaper Zone | Wild Card Zone |
| **Low** | Ant Colony Zone | Strategic Rat Hole |

Relative Uncertainty
**Low**                              **High**

# Legend:

**Wallpaper Zone:** High impact/low uncertainty. Like wallpaper, factors here are often ignored, but can be very powerful.

**Ant Colony Zone:** Low impact/low uncertainty. As with ant colonies, many of these factors put together can create substantial advantages.

**Wild Card Zone:** High impact/high uncertainty. As in a jokers-wild poker game, these are unpredictable factors that can work massively in your favor—or against it.

**Strategic Rat Hole:** Low impact/high uncertainty. Like any other rat hole, a place you'd rather not be.

All together, this is a curious kind of map. The opportunities indicated on the left side—the Wallpaper and Ant Colony Zones—are inherently attractive because of their low uncertainty risk. The Wallpaper Zone is especially attractive; factors that have low uncertainty and high impact provide the basis for bets with the best risk/return profiles. The task on this side of the map, which we tackle in step 8, is to see and capitalize on these factors *before* your competition does. Yet, and this is the curious part, both of these zones, and particularly the Wallpaper one, are routinely ignored, just as wallpaper in a house often is—and hence the name for this quadrant.

The opportunities on the right side of the map—the Wild Card and Strategic Rat Hole Zones—lead to an inverse set of curiosities. People pay a lot of attention to the factors in these zones, investing in both elegant and detailed analyses and in bold macho bets, despite higher levels of risk for equivalent payoffs compared to the left side of the map. But the real task in these zones, which we focus on in step 9, is to determine whether you need to be on this side of the map at all, and to the extent that you do, to figure out how to move to the left and lessen the inherent risks or up the returns for the risks being taken.

\* \* \* \*

So, say it's early April 1775, and you're in Boston with Paul Revere and the other rebel leaders. You know you have very limited time and resources, especially relative to the British forces. You also know that it's essential to map the future space quickly so you can figure out the ways with the best odds for keeping the British from capturing your leaders and most of your weaponry.

But here's the problem: You only have a mishmash of conclusions and data and info scraps. You're almost certain that the British are going to attack, with the goal of breaking the back of the incipient rebellion. You don't know when exactly, but it's probably soon. When the British attack, you think they are going to hit Lexington first, to capture Samuel Adams and John Hancock, and then go on to Concord to confiscate your main weapons stash. You don't know whether they are going to deploy their troops by land or by sea. You also don't know how many men they will bring, but you reckon it's going to be more than you will be able to muster. You are pretty sure about how the British will fight, though: in lines and in red uniforms, because that's the way they've always done it and you've seen no evidence that would lead you to think that this time would be different.

How would you organize this mess of data into a picture you could use as a help in thinking about how to allocate your scarce resources into your next set of bets?

This is our version:

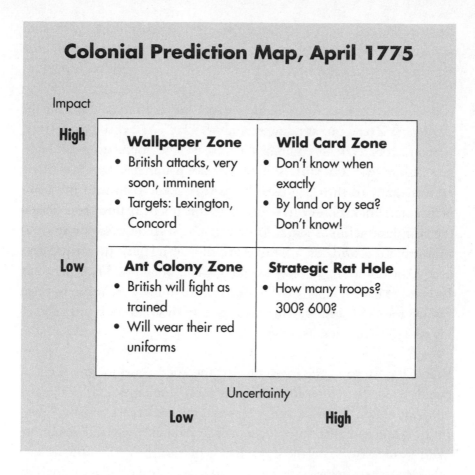

**Colonial Prediction Map, April 1775**

Impact

| | **Wallpaper Zone** | **Wild Card Zone** |
|---|---|---|
| **High** | • British attacks, very soon, imminent<br>• Targets: Lexington, Concord | • Don't know when exactly<br>• By land or by sea? Don't know! |
| **Low** | **Ant Colony Zone**<br>• British will fight as trained<br>• Will wear their red uniforms | **Strategic Rat Hole**<br>• How many troops? 300? 600? |

Uncertainty

Low                                    High

And here's a fast tour of the map:

Wallpaper Factors. We start with the Wallpaper factors, because they are the sweet spot of any Prediction Map: high impact and low uncertainty. Whether the potential impact of these factors is positive or negative, the power of identifying the Wallpaper factors comes from the *value of certainty*. Revere and company knew that if they did nothing, their ability to establish a new republic would be diminished, perhaps to almost nothing; they also knew that if they acted, they'd have a shot at keeping their cause alive and even pushing it forward. Paul Revere and his colleagues may not have been happy that an attack on Lexington and Concord was impending, *but knowing that this assault was highly likely was valuable because it allowed them to focus their scarce resources* on two critical and linked goals—first on figuring out when the attack would take place and then on foiling it.

**Ant Colony Factors.** Ant Colony factors are similar to those in the Wallpaper Zone, but at a lower volume. Like ants working together, these factors can be combined to create the foundation of high-payoff/low-risk strategies, in effect creating bundles of Ant Colony factors that can then be pushed upward on the map into the high-impact territory. As in the Wallpaper Zone, even neutral or negative Ant Colony factors, such as knowing that your adversary will wear bright red uniforms on a bleak April morning (and, trust us, almost every April morning in New England is bleak) and will fight in a line formation, have the potential to be assets if you pay attention to them (which the colonists, wearing scrungy and drab attire, did by shooting and then running into the woods).

**Wild Card Factors.** Next we come to the Wild Card factors. Lots of people (and, therefore, lots of companies) think that the Wallpaper and Ant Colony factors, being reasonably predictable, are by definition boring and therefore not worthy of much time and attention. Wild Card factors, on the other hand, due to their high impact and inherent uncertainties, are plenty interesting, especially to analysts whose job it is to analyze such things. The job of the smart gambler, on the other hand, is to lessen this uncertainty risk—sidestep it, avoid it, lessen it, or hedge it; the one thing you shouldn't do is accept it with the same payoffs you could get with a less risky bet. Paul Revere and his colleagues couldn't sidestep their Wild Card factors, but they did push them a bit to the left of the map by investing some of their scarce resources in gaining more certainty (that "one if by land, and two if by sea" thing that the colonists used to signal, via lamps in a church belfry, whether and how the British were launching their attack).

**Strategic Rat Hole Factors.** And finally there are the Strategic Rat Hole factors. These are the business and personal equivalents of the old ecclesiastical arguments about how many angels could dance on the head of a pin. These factors may not have nearly as much impact as the other factors on what you are trying to achieve but the uncertainty is so high that you can spend endless hours debating them, which is why we call them Strategic Rat Holes. Once Revere and his comrades had decided to take a stand on the Lexington and Concord battlefields, determining the precise number of troops that would line up against them would have been a poor use of scarce resources. If you only have so much time before you have to place your bets, are you better off refining estimates that are important but not critical, or sharpening your plans to deal with those factors that could make the biggest difference to your future?

## CONSTRUCTING THE MAPS USING THE SANTA METHOD

Constructing a Prediction Map is relatively straightforward. As in the Christmas carol, we follow the same process that Santa is said to use to make his decisions about which children get Christmas gifts and which don't—we make a list and then we check it twice (and sometimes even more often). Unlike Santa, though, we don't care who's been naughty or who's been nice; our lists focus only on degrees of impact and uncertainty.

Here's how we make our lists. First, we define the time frame. For Paul Revere, sitting in Boston in 1775, the time frame was days or weeks, not months or years. If you are deciding whether to invest in a new compound that might have the potential to be a blockbuster drug (or, conversely, to soak up hundreds of millions of dollars in development costs and return nothing), your time frame will be years— a decade or more. For most corporate strategy decisions, we find a time frame of three to five years works best.

Then we define what we mean by the term *future impacts of external factors*, the inputs for creating Prediction Maps. For corporate groups, we usually define these as "factors *outside* your company's direct control." We do this for the simple reason that otherwise the first twenty "external" factors listed will be variants of "those idiots above us make the following boneheaded moves." Sometimes we do a second pass looking at future impacts of internal factors as a way to identify internal implementation and organizational issues for a given set of bets. Whichever way you decide to proceed, it's essential to be clear on how you define the factors that you are using as the basis for your maps.

With all this in hand, we set to work, using the following process:

1. First list all the factors you believe will or could have major future impacts on the objectives you wish to achieve. For this step especially, putting your thoughts in writing is really important; otherwise you are likely to miss something or forget a thought that will turn out to be significant. It's also important to go fast—even for corporate groups, we find that fifteen to thirty minutes can be enough time to generate a great first draft of this list. Don't worry about whether all thoughts are fully fleshed out or written in parallel form; just get out an initial list and go fast.

2. Once you have the first-draft list of the high-impact factors, sort them by how high the future impact is likely to be. You might use a scale of big deal, super big deal, and ultracritical big deal; or you might use a 0-to-10 scale where 0 is the lowest impact and 10 is the highest (since your base list is already the high-impact factors, effectively the scale will turn out to range only from about 6 to 10). This sort by impact will give you the vertical axis for the Prediction Map.

3. Then, sort the factors by degree of uncertainty. If you can express the factor as a statement—"Personal computers and mobile phones will continue to get smaller and have more features," or "A substantial portion of the population is overweight and these numbers will grow"—you probably have a factor that you believe to have low uncertainty. Conversely, if a factor is easily expressed as a question to which you're not sure you have the answer—"Will we go to a single-payer health insurance system?" or "What are oil prices going to do

over the next several years?"—chances are you have a factor with high uncertainty. This sort by uncertainty gives the horizontal axis for the map.

**4.** Check the impact estimates. In the spirit of Santa, we think of this as the up-and-down Sanity check (up-and-down for the vertical axis of the Prediction Map, which shows degree of impact), relooking at what possible implications the factor or group of factors could hold for you or your company.

Consider these three factors: baby boomers getting older; baby boomers still as vain as ever or even vainer; and men's and women's physiques shift in pretty predictable ways over the years (that gravity thing again). If you are an apparel maker, the implication you might draw from these factors in combination is . . . fashionable clothes styles designed for aging boomers could be one big honking market, and you might in consequence move this group of factors higher on your map.

**5.** Check the uncertainty estimates. We think of this one as the left-and-right sanity check (left-and-right for the horizontal axis that shows degree of uncertainty), looking especially at the rationale for why you think this factor or group of factors is a relatively sure thing—or why, on the other hand, you think it is one that might resolve in a number of different ways.

When Billy Beane advocated using "walks drawn" by college baseball players as a selection criterion, for example, most of his colleagues thought this would be a poor way to spot future talent. But Beane's rationale, based on the data, is compelling: the more walks a college player draws, the better he controls the strike zone, which indicates a better chance of getting on base, which in turn ups the odds for more runs and ultimately more wins. Rather than belonging on the far-right/high-uncertainty side of the map, Beane and others of his analytic ilk would argue, this factor should be placed on the left.

Even more important in many cases is to do the left-and-right sanity check on factors that you've already placed on the left side. Lots of companies, jobs, and marriages have been lost when one party assigns too much certainty to the other party putting up with mediocrity or worse—in products, work efforts, or day-to-day give-and-take. The left-and-right sanity check won't prevent this outcome, of course, but it does give you another prompt to think hard about how sure you are about the factors you've put on the left side of the map.

6. Put the factors on the grid, take a look at the first draft of your Prediction Map and do a final "common-sense" check. If the map seems wrong to you, ask what seems to be surprising, fool around with the variables, and push yourself to do a second (fast!) draft.

\* \* \*

Santa, as far as we can tell, has never lost sight of why he's making lists of which girls and boys have been naughty and which have been nice—he's getting ready for his Christmas gift run and he wants to make sure the right children get the right toys.

The same discipline goes for Prediction Maps. The purpose of these maps is to help you see emerging patterns fast—whether you're creating the maps to craft and refine a corporate strategy, or to decide who to hire or promote or discipline or fire, or to aid in a major career and life decision about whether to stay in a company or leave. Then you can make better predictions about future consequences of alternative paths of action—while you still have the time to create bets that have better odds of getting you where you want to go in *the context of how the world is likely to be*, rather than how it is now or how you would prefer it to be. And every time you create bets that have better odds, you are making your own luck.

Trying to construct a perfect Prediction Map misses the point— this is a race that goes to the swift. As John Boyd might have said, knowing with absolute certainty that the enemy is going to successfully shoot you dead right now is probably not as valuable as seeing that the enemy is about to be in position to shoot you dead and getting out of the way fast (and, if you were John Boyd, then getting yourself positioned on his tail so you could shoot him instead).

## THE PERPLEXED PROFESSOR

*A company uses a written test graded on a fixed curve to make its final hiring decisions on a group of 60 candidates who have already made it through all the other screens.*

*The hiring rules work out like this: the top 9 performers on the test get the plum jobs; the bottom 9 get a thank you and a good-bye; and the remaining 42 get jobs throughout the company that are good but not as good as the ones for the top performers.*

*The evaluator has already assigned all but two of the ratings and must now decide:*

- *who gets the remaining average rating and a job, and*
- *who gets the low rating and no job.*

*Her decision comes down to performance on a complex math question, one that is pertinent to the kinds of calculations done by professionals in this company. Candidate 1 got the right answer, but worksheets accompanying the answer are confusing and garbled. Candidate 2 got the wrong answer, but his worksheets show a fundamental understanding of the underlying principles marred by a couple of computational mistakes on several of the interim steps.*

*Which candidate should get the job offer and why?*

___ *Candidate 1, the one who got the right answer but had confusing and garbled worksheets, should get the job offer.*

___ *Candidate 2, the one who got the wrong answer but had strong worksheets marred by a couple of computational errors, should get the offer.*

*Why?* _____

## The Gambler's Dozen, Step 8

# WALLPAPER JUJITSU:
## Focus on What's Certain

# The Gospel According to Preston Sturges

IN Hollywood, in the 1940s, Preston Sturges was The Man. Okay, maybe not the ultimate go-to guy, but with an Oscar and string of hits, he was certainly one of moviedom's movers and shakers.

Perhaps Sturges had grown tired of aspiring cineastes coming to him for advice. Or maybe, like many high achievers, he wanted to codify his formula for success. Whatever the reason, Sturges boiled down his film-making recipe to this list:

- A pretty girl is better than an ugly one.
- A leg is better than an arm.
- A bedroom is better than a living room.
- An arrival is better than a departure.
- A birth is better than a death.
- A chase is better than a chat.
- A dog is better than a landscape.
- A kitten is better than a dog.
- A baby is better than a kitten.
- A kiss is better than a baby.
- A pratfall is better than anything else.

So, let's say you're the agent representing an actor who has been box-office magic in most every comedy he or she has played in—an Adam Sandler perhaps, or a Cameron Diaz—but pretty much box-office poison in every drama.

Now say your client wants to show that he or she has the chops to do the serious stuff, and has instructed you to find one of those heavy, deep and real roles. Do you send a copy of Sturges's list to your client? And, if you were the client, would you follow it, and why?

# 8. Wallpaper Jujitsu: What Are My Best "Left Side" Bets?

JACK Welch has broken the code on culture change. And he did it, we believe, using the eighth skill of Predictive Intelligence, figuring out how to leverage the power and momentum of the factors on the left side of the Prediction Map into bets that will get you where you want to go with the least risk. And where Jack Welch wanted to go was higher sales, higher profits, and a higher stock price.

It may be difficult to believe now, but when Welch took over General Electric in 1981, GE was a very large, sleepy, high-prestige, grow-with-the-GNP type of place with a stock price to match. And when you have well close to half a million employees, as GE did in those days, inertia alone is enough to keep you a sleepy, high-prestige, grow-with-the-GNP type of place, no matter who steps into the top job.

Unless that person is Jack Welch.

Because what Welch knew is that culture change can be achieved relatively quickly and reliably if you do it right. In the spirit of Preston Sturges, we've boiled down Welch's approach to culture change, GE-style, into these eight simple rules: (1) decide what the company is going to achieve; (2) tell everyone; (3) decide what metrics correlate best with the goals; (4) tell everyone; (5) measure business units on how well they perform against the goals; (6) tell everyone; (7) reward the winners and punish the losers extravagantly; (8) tell everyone.

Welch might not have articulated his rules this way back then, and might not even today. But watching him from the outside, this is what he appears to have done. And, in less than three years, Welch

transformed GE from an elegant, sleep-inducing kind of conglomer-
ate into an aggressive, mean, high-performance monster. And with
the result he intended, we would say; from 1981, when Welch took
over, to 2001, when he retired, the company's market cap increased
about thirtyfold.

One way to understand what Welch did and how he did it is to look
at the Wallpaper Zone for GE in 1981. Our version looks like this:

## Wallpaper Zone, GE Prediction Map, 1981

Impact

**High**

- Stock price will go up as earnings and revenues go up
- Fundamentals of many GE businesses—GE Credit Corp, Lightbulb, Plastics, others—very strong; can support far better performance
- Growth fundamentals of some GE businesses weak—e.g., Housewares, others—will continue to be a drag on corporate performance
- GE wealth and prestige will allow company to continue to attract great people
- Our people will do what is measured and what is rewarded (just like everyone at every other company)
- GE's current measures/rewards, if left in place, will lead to cautious, about-average corporate performance

Relative Uncertainty

**Low**

In effect, Welch's move to transform GE's culture and performance leveraged these Wallpaper factors. This in turn allowed him to revolutionize the company and how it did business without worrying about the kinds of uncertainties that other executives often fret over when they are trying to make these kinds of changes; who would survive, for example, or what the patterns for "mourning"—the time, according to some experts, employees need to "grieve" over the death of the old ways of doing things—would be.

That's because Welch defined the new game such that those who played well would do well and so would the corporation, and those who didn't wish to play—or played poorly, or needed time to mourn—would leave. As with the eastern sport of Jujitsu, Welch derived power from the weight and strength of the Wallpaper factors to get the results he wanted with the least amount of risk, creating what we think of as "Wallpaper Jujitsu."

Figuring out how to leverage the factors on the left side of the Prediction Map into effective and relatively low-risk bets is the purpose of this step, which fits in the PA—Predict and Act!—part of the OOPA! process. For this step, we look at two kinds of left-side bets: those you can create when you first enter a situation, and those you re-create when you are willing to revise a current set of bets to take better advantage of existing Wallpaper factors. Then, for both, we recommend a quick empathy test to understand the motives of the other players so we can assess whether the proposed "left-side" bet that may look so certain on first inspection might actually be more of a trap than an opportunity.

## FOCUS ON WHAT'S CERTAIN: CREATING THE LEFT-SIDE BETS

Do you know where your best left-side bets are? The answer to this question will depend a lot on two factors.

The first factor is your goals. Going back to the world of movies and movie stars, if you are Cameron Diaz or Adam Sandler, do you want to be even richer, or do you want more prestige? If your answer is that you want to increase your wealth and you believe that Sturges's advice is still at least directionally correct for comedic actors, then the Gospel According to Preston Sturges could aid you in finding your best left-side bets. But if your goal is truly more prestige even if it puts you back financially, then advice about pratfalls probably won't be helpful to you.

The second factor is your field of vision and whether you can see the Wallpaper factors that could help you achieve your goals with the least risk. Oddly, many people either don't see the Wallpaper factors at all or pass up the bets that make use of them. Remember General McClellan at Antietam? He passed on the perfect Wallpaper bet. Or think about the thousands of companies that turned "change management" into a lifelong, largely unsuccessful but very expensive set of projects. Translating clear goals into consistent metrics and rewards, as Jack Welch did at GE, is a much safer and more effective set of bets.

Or consider what Bill Gates and Microsoft did in the late 1970s and early 1980s to establish the company in what was then a new industry—desktop computing.

## New Left-Side Bets: Microsoft and the PC Business

If you were born in the 1960s or after, you may not be able to imagine the business world as it was in 1980. IBM was a huge power, bigger even than GE by a factor of more than two, and more powerful, enough so to have triggered a nasty and prolonged antitrust suit, courtesy of the U.S. government. Relative to IBM, Microsoft wasn't a flea on an elephant's rump, it was an atom of a molecule of a speck on the flea's rump.

Desktop computing was just beginning then, and a lot of people, including a lot of very smart people, thought the idea of a small computer dedicated to a single user was a fad or a flash in the pan. Others took the opposite point of view, and soon there were all sorts of boxes from all sorts of hardware companies—Commodores, and Osbornes, and Timex Sinclairs, and TRSs from Tandy, and Apples too (but not yet the Mac, that came in 1984)—each with its own operating system, often variants of CP/M from a company called Digital Research Inc.

By 1980, IBM had determined that the second camp was right and, accordingly, had started a top-secret project to develop its entry into the market, which it launched a year later as the "IBM 5150 Personal Computer." To save time and money, the company decided to outsource the microprocessors, operating system, and other key applications for the 5150.

So, say it's 1980 and you're Bill Gates, college dropout and chairman and president of the then-minuscule Microsoft Corporation, which you incorporated four years before. You think that the market for personal computers will be bigger and grow faster than even IBM understands, and your goal is to dominate this new industry. You also understand that you may have credibility with IBM through your mother's connections to IBM's president, John Opel. What do you predict will be the best path to grow your company and move closer to your goal?

What follows is how we imagine the top half of Bill Gates's Prediction Map would have looked like at that time.

# The (Imaginary) Bill Gates Prediction Map, early PC era

Impact

**High**

| **Wallpaper Zone** | **Wild Card Zone** |
|---|---|
| • Too many hardware makers; shakeout coming, many will die | • Will applications drive purchase decisions (by customers) or hardware design (by competitors)? |
| • IBM entering the market and will survive shakeout | • Will there be a dominant hardware configuration? Or a dominate hardware/OS configuration? |
| • Market growing bigger, faster than IBM understands | |
| • Applications must be compatible with operating systems | • Will IBM be winner or just a player in hardware arena? |
| • CP/M operating system is a force to be dealt with but is not yet winner | • Don't know which operating system will dominate—will it be CP/M or other? |
| • Apple is going to keep its operating system closed | |
| • Mom on United Way board with John Opel (IBM president) | |

Relative Uncertainty

**Low**                              **High**

Oh, and did we mention that at the time Microsoft did not actually have an operating system to sell?

What most companies did in these early days of the PC industry, and what is commonly seen in the early stages of any new technology, was to come at the problem from the right (high-uncertainty) side of the Prediction Map and try to win by developing the best box or the best operating system—faster, easier, cheaper, slicker. Bets like this are right-side bets because their success depends on how one or more critical uncertainties will play out—in this case, what the market will consider "the best" and what customers will be willing to pay for.

That's not what Gates and Microsoft did, however. Instead they based their betting approach on the left (low-uncertainty) side of the Prediction Map, leveraging the Wallpaper factors to set the de facto standard for the industry, fast, by grabbing control of the operating system.

Here's how they did it. The first piece was IBM, where Gates had more than the usual access for a tiny start-up, no matter how brainy, due to his mother's connections to John Opel. IBM was important because, whatever happened in this market, IBM was going to be a player—maybe the leader, maybe not—but in either case an important participant. Then the task for Microsoft was to carry out its end of the deal and get the right terms in return.

In the actual case, Microsoft did convince IBM that it could deliver the goods despite not actually having an operating system to sell at the time. And it got the right terms; as Gates later recalled, "a key point in our [Microsoft's] negotiation with IBM was making sure that we could license to other manufacturers." As for the operating system itself, Microsoft solved that problem by acquiring the rights to something called the Quick and Dirty Operating System that, after being acquired and further developed by Microsoft, became first known as PC-DOS and soon thereafter as, you guessed it, MS-DOS.

This ability to license the operating system to others then allowed Microsoft to go to the other hardware manufacturers and argue that they should have two operating systems—their own and the DOS system—and lots of them did, because . . . well . . . because IBM did.

And finally, Microsoft opened its code to all applications developers, which meant more applications worked with DOS, which meant more users bought DOS-based computers, which meant . . .

Which meant that Microsoft won no matter what happened with the Wild Card factors. Instead of trying to build a better mousetrap, which has plenty of risk and is what Microsoft's competitors did, Gates and his company went for ubiquity, and they used the Wallpaper factors to get there.

## Revised Left-Side Bets: Landmark and the Cable TV Business

We suppose that one moral of the Gates story might be to beware of geeks bearing gifts. But the real moral is to focus on the left and the factors that you are relatively certain about, because the more you can leverage the Wallpaper factors, the better shot you have of creating the bets that will get you closer to the goals you have set for yourself with the least amount of risk.

Often creating good Wallpaper bets isn't a matter of creating brand-new bets, as Gates did. Instead, the key is to alter bets currently in place. That's what Jack Welch did at GE when he leveraged a combination of Wallpaper factors to change the internal rules at GE.

It's also what happened in the early days at the Weather Channel, the brainchild of privately held Landmark Communications.

The economics of television programming, like those of many other media businesses, are based on advertising revenues. The basis for Landmark's bet on the Weather Channel, launched in 1981, was that its new venture would be able to grab a 2 to 3 percent share of cable advertising. But by 1984, the Weather Channel was caught in a Catch-22. National advertisers didn't think weather would draw viewers. And A. C. Nielsen, which provided the audience ratings that could show that people were watching, wouldn't provide ratings for a cable network until it had penetrated at least 15 percent of TV households nationwide.

This Catch-22 would have killed the Weather Channel had there not been other, even more fundamental factors at work: Cable capacity was expanding faster than the content available to fill it. New capacity was very expensive to build, which meant the operators needed to borrow money, and lots of it. But if the cable operators didn't find the kind of programming people in their viewing areas were willing to pay for, investment professionals would see these ventures as more risky, and that would mean increased financing costs for the cable operators. And finally, the cable operators were discovering that local viewers liked the Weather Channel—a lot. Maybe not as much as ESPN, but enough to make it valuable to the operators.

Looking back, this combination of Wallpaper factors may explain why Landmark's last-ditch effort, which was to charge the operators a low subscriber fee of five cents per subscriber per month to carry the Weather Channel, worked and saved the enterprise. As one of the cable operators said at the time, "You know, we're going to say yes to your proposal to pay fees. . . . And that's because Wall Street and the investment community figure that the thing that will drive cable is differentiated programming. We're expecting to have to borrow hundreds of millions from lenders, and it's cheaper to pay you than to take yet another interest-rate increase."

In effect, what Landmark had done was to construct a Wallpaper strategy that let both sides—the operators and the Weather Channel—win, and all the operators agreed to the plan. Today, the Weather Channel is one of the most valuable, and valued, franchises in television.

## USE EMPATHY TO TEST FOR TRAPS

Not all bets are as good as they first appear. Or as Trojan priest Laocoon put it some 3,000 years ago when he and his fellow citizens of Troy saw a gigantic wooden horse outside the city gates, "*Timeo Danaos et dona ferentes.*" The rough translation is "Beware of Greeks bearing gifts." We think a better lesson is to use the power of empathy to test the Wallpaper bets from the other party's point of view, before taking final action.

If your memory of the classics is rusty (or you're depending on the movie rendition), here's the short version. The Greeks and Trojans had been at war for over ten years. The Trojans had stolen Helen, the most beautiful woman in the world, from her husband, King Menelaus. The Greeks were fighting to get her back, and losing, because the ancient city of Troy was well fortified and almost impervious to attack.

That's when the horse showed up, outside the city gates. You know the rest of the story. The Trojans interpreted the horse as a peace offering from the Greeks, and promptly celebrated with lots of drinking and dancing and, after that, more drinking still. But though it looked like the Greeks had headed home, they had in fact withdrawn their ships only beyond the horizon, taking all their warriors with them except for the few they had sealed in the belly of the horse. At nightfall, when the Trojans were too drunk to notice, the soldiers who had hidden in the horse let themselves out, quietly went around the perimeter of the city walls killing all the sentries, and then opened the gates for the rest of the Greeks, who had returned to Troy under cover of darkness. By morning, the Greeks had Helen back, and all the Trojans were either dead or enslaved.

The Greeks, of course, had executed Wallpaper Jujitsu, using the Trojans' dual preference for keeping Helen and getting rid of the Greeks as the power source for their sneak attack. Not all Wallpaper bets have such catastrophic impacts on the counterparties, of course (though some companies that built applications based on DOS may now feel more kinship with the Trojans in this story than with the Greeks). But in general, using empathy can help you assess if there's a significant gap between the way the opportunity looks to you and your empathetic understanding of the other side's situation and goals. If there is a gap and it's big, watch out; if it's small, you may have a good bet.

An approach like that might have helped the Trojans. Then they would have remembered that the Greeks felt only hatred and rage toward the Trojans at the time they left the horse: hatred and rage that the Trojans had stolen Helen, that the great Greek army couldn't beat the Trojans, and that the war had dragged on for ten years without a successful resolution. Why, given that kind of underlying emotional map, would the Greeks now give up and go away? At minimum, such an empathy check done by the Trojans might have suggested that the horse was a Wild Card bet for them rather than a Wallpaper one, and that maybe they ought to modify their response accordingly, a topic we address in more detail in the next step.

The flip is true for the cable operators looking at the deal that Landmark proposed. In that case, Landmark actually opened its books and showed the operators the complete financial picture for the Weather Channel, making it easy for the cable operators to do an empathy check on Landmark's motives. With the numbers in hand, the cable operators could see straight into Landmark's situation and understand the company's short- and longer-term goals for the Weather Channel. In consequence, both Landmark and the operators were able to use the Wallpaper factors to structure a bet that gave both sides more of what they wanted with less risk—definitely our kind of bet.

John Boyd emphasized empathy as an important part of military strategy, as we do for corporate ones and personal ones. One use is to be able to forecast what an adversary will do fast enough to be able to move in advance and into superior position, as the Greeks did to the Trojans. Another is to understand the potential areas of shared interests and thereby craft viable alliances, as Landmark did with the cable operators. The point in either case is not to identify with partners or adversaries, but rather to *understand the world from their point of view well enough to make intelligent predictions about what they are likely to do next and under what conditions*—which improves your bets by taking some of the uncertainty, and therefore some of the risk, out of the gambles.

\* \* \* \*

Wallpaper factors describe the most likely key conditions and rules of the future space you will be playing in, and bets that leverage these factors therefore give you the biggest bang for the buck with the least uncertainty about how the future will unfold. Smart gamblers invest a good portion of their 100 marbles here, either to ride a wave that will help them achieve a goal or to deal with a situation they don't like but understand is on the way. In either case, they make their own luck by "betting with the house"—aligning themselves with the new rules and working to take or create as much advantage of these new rules as they can to get closer to the outcomes they want to achieve.

## THE DEMENTED GENIE RETURNS

*You're sitting on the beach one day, and suddenly a genie, the slightly demented one you had met previously, appears before you again.*

*"Howdy," says the genie. "You get three more wishes."*

*"What's the catch?" you say.*

*"No catch," the genie replies. "It's just that whatever you wish, your ex-partner, the person you hate most in this world, will get the same, tenfold."*

*"Okay," you say. You think about it for a bit, and then you ask for a lovely ocean-front estate on an acre of land.*

*Done. And when you see it, you can't believe your eyes. So then you ask for furnishings and paintings and beautiful landscaping, and as soon as the words leave your lips, you realize that you've just used up your second wish.*

*"Ah," says the genie. "I've done what you've asked, but you may have forgotten the condition—and you do realize, don't you, that your ex now has an even more beautiful estate, on ten acres, with French antiques rather than your country pine ones, and where you have great art by local artists, your ex now has Cezannes, and Monets, and even a Picasso?"*

*And with that the genie asks you for your third and final wish.*

*What do you wish for?*

# The Gambler's Dozen, Step 9

# RISK SPLITS:
# Reduce the Uncertainties

# Sidewalk Games

YOU'RE in New York City one day, or Paris, or Hong Kong. You come across a street game in which a player is tossing a coin. He has just tossed ten straight heads. He invites you to bet on the next toss of the coin at even odds, and indicates that you can choose the amount of money to lay down on the bet. He throws the coin into the air. What bet do you call?

# 9. Risks Splits: How Much Risk Can I Shed or Shift?

ONE thing we can say about street games, and it's true whether the dealer comes from the Bronx, the Marais, or Kowloon: once you decide to play, you are deep into the right-side territory of the Prediction Map.

If you are the passerby, you have three choices. You can assume that the coin is loaded, and will therefore land heads-side up the next time too. If you make that prediction, you'll take the bet and put your money on heads.

Or you could assume that the dealer is trying to trick you. In that case, you might predict that he will predict that you will pick heads, so you then guess that the next toss will therefore likely be tails. In that case, you could take the bet and put your money on tails.

Or, you could be like us, and bug out of this situation as fast as you could.

\*    \*    \*    \*

No matter what the situation, you always want to know the game you're playing. And not only that, as much as you can, you want to be the person who knows the rules of the game being played and, even better, to be the person who controls these rules. That's why we love the Wallpaper bets; the less uncertainty we have about the future impact of factors beyond our control, the more we understand the rules and the better we can construct bets that use these rules to get us closer to where we want to be.

In the case of the sidewalk game, there are two arguments for how to bet if you are going to stay in the game—one for calling heads and the other for calling tails. Both are plausible and either *could* be true, but it's equally possible that either one is wrong too. These are the uncertainties that put you on the right side of the Prediction Map.

Navigating the right side of the Prediction Map is a fact of life, in business as well as out. The key, and the skill on which this step of the Gambler's Dozen is based, is to find ways to structure bets that reduce the risk of taking the wrong side of the wager. This again is a PA—Predict and Act!—skill, which we exercise in two pieces. First, before we bet, we decompose the situation to understand the underlying uncertainties and associated potential costs as a tool for figuring out if we have to play or even want to play. Then, if we decide to bet, we restructure the wagers to reduce or redistribute as much of the risk as we can, unless we are getting a disproportionate reward for the risks we are taking.

## DECOMPOSE FIRST: OUTCOMES, ODDS, AND CONSEQUENCES

Risky situations are sneaky. Typically you see the bets before you see the underlying uncertainties; a big wooden horse appears outside the city gates, or a street vendor proposes a game of chance. Before you bet, a few moments' thought about the one or two dominant uncertainties and the associated odds and consequences can pay big dividends.

In many cases, a single uncertainty or a set of highly correlated factors that can be treated as a single uncertainty dominates. For the big horse the Trojans find courtesy of the departing Greeks, the dominant Wild Card factor is whether the horse is truly what it seems, an extravagant gift, or whether it is a trick.

A simple picture of this uncertainty would look like this:

**Horse is a gift ◄————► Horse is a trick**

If the horse is a gift, the consequences of this outcome aren't that great really because if the Greeks aren't playing a trick on you, the horse is just a horse (though a very big one). But, if you tried the empathy test from step 8, you should at least question how high the odds are that the horse is what it first appears to be, a gift from the departing and now vanquished Greeks.

On the other hand, if the horse is a trick, the consequences for you are huge, because then the horse could be part of a secret plot aimed at harming you. Even with small odds of this being so, the consequences are so large that developing an alternate plan to an immediate drunken celebration might be the better part of valor. What would have happened, do you think, if the Trojan elders had invented a three-day purification ritual especially for the horse that would have kept it isolated and the townspeople sober for long enough to at least think about Laocoon's warning, the one about not trusting the Greek warriors even when they bring gifts?

In the case of the street game, say you think the game is rigged but you also think you're hip to all that and you decide it would be fun to try to outsmart the dealer. Then you might assume that the coin used for the eleventh toss is loaded and in consequence think about two critical uncertainties: (1) whether the coin for this toss is loaded for heads or loaded for tails, and (2) whether the dealer will just throw the coin or use sleight-of-hand or other tricks to control the results of the toss. Now we can lay these two uncertainties against each other in an Uncertainty Grid to see the four possible outcomes of taking the dealer's bet, based on the two uncertainties we think will govern the situation.

# Uncertainty Grid: Outcomes on the Street Game

**Will use sleight-of-hand to switch coins**

| | | |
|---|---|---|
| **This coin weighted for heads** | 4. Dealer's choice | 3. Dealer's choice |
| | 1. You win if you bet heads | 2. You win if you bet tails |

**This coin weighted for tails**

**Will not use a sleight-of-hand**

What's clear when you look at this grid is that the dealer knows the rules and you don't, and therefore that the odds are steeply in the dealer's favor. You could win with heads, and you could win with tails, or you could win with either if the dealer decides to play you by letting you win a few times, and then, when the ante has gotten higher, enticing you into a game of double or nothing. The consequences of these outcomes depend on the stakes and your circumstances; trivial if you are betting your beer money and you enjoy the rush of matching wits with an expert, substantial if you are betting the rent money or are a recently reformed compulsive gambler.

There's an old saying at the poker tables that applies equally to street games, business games, and life games: if you can't spot the sucker at the table, odds are . . . it's you. For this reason, and as much as possible, you want to be the person who knows the rules of the game being played. When you don't, and you have the choice, you want to opt out of the play. Decomposing the bet is one quick way to sketch out the potential outcomes, odds, and consequences, so you can decide whether to play, bug out, or go a step further and restructure the bet.

## RESTRUCTURE NEXT: REDUCE OR REALLOCATE THE RISK

In many cases, opting out isn't a viable option because you can't get close enough to the future you're trying to create without placing bets based on factors on the right side of the Prediction Map. In these situations, we construct grids like the one we did for the street game to begin our process of figuring out if we can restructure our bets and how. We then use these grids to spark ideas for ways to shift, share, or sidestep the underlying uncertainties and therefore reduce our risk that we will end up with much worse outcomes than we planned on.

Mechanically, this is pretty straightforward. Go back to the Wild Card factors you developed in step 7, pick the two you think will have the biggest impact on your future and that are reasonably independent of each other (so you don't end up with two flavors of the same factor—like "frost hits orange crop" and "price of oranges goes up"), and construct an Uncertainty Grid. Play around with the pairs until you get a picture that feels like it captures some of the risks and upsides you are facing. Up to this point, if you've ever done traditional scenario planning, you'll recognize these mechanics as similar to what you did in that process, with two key differences. One is that we move fast, constructing our grids and using them for decisions in a matter of minutes or hours as opposed to months or years. The other is the question we ask after we've got a first draft of the grid.

We ask the same question for each of the four quadrants, either going over each one by one and writing down our answers or, if we're working in a group, dividing the group into four smaller teams, one per quadrant. Our question is this: *if three years from now (or whatever the right time frame is) you found that this situation was the one that actually did come to pass, what bets would you then wish that you had made now?*

With this question, you can then look at the bets you would have wished to have placed and compare them with what you are actually doing or are planning to do at present. If your current bets fit only one of the quadrants, pay attention; you're playing a high-risk game that two of the key uncertainties you've identified will resolve in the way you desire. And, if you've assumed that these one-quadrant-only bets are "obvious" or "no-brainers," watch out; you are taking highly risky bets without appreciating the degree of risk that you've signed on for.

Using this kind of bet assessment and restructuring works when you see new risks and you know that you'll need to respond to these new risks by changing your bets. It also works when the risks were there the whole time but you either didn't see them or couldn't figure out ways to sidestep them earlier. In either case you'll have to restructure the bets you initially made, which may be a lot easier to do once you remember that betting is a forward activity and that being right or wrong yesterday is irrelevant to the bets you place today.

## Responding to New Risks: The PC Business, Post MS-DOS

An example of new bets in response to new risks is the PC industry at the time that IBM introduced the 5150 with Microsoft's DOS operating system. Say you were a top executive at one of the other companies (besides IBM and Apple) that were already participating or wanting to participate in this new industry in the early 1980s. In this situation, you might have picked these two critical uncertainties based on IBM's entry into the market with a Microsoft operating system:

1. whether the adoption rate for the PC would be rather slow (as many analysts and IBM were predicting), or whether it would go fast; and
2. whether the new operating system, DOS, that this new company, Microsoft, was pitching to all the hardware vendors would continue to be just one of many, or whether it would become the industry standard and the one that all applications would need to be compatible with.

Your Uncertainty Grid might then look like this:

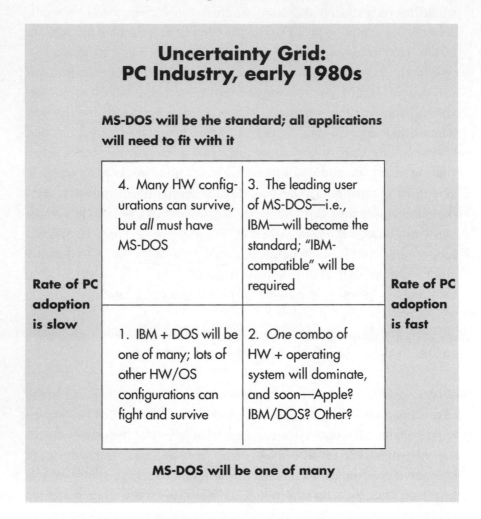

# Uncertainty Grid:
# PC Industry, early 1980s

**MS-DOS will be the standard; all applications will need to fit with it**

|  |  |
|---|---|
| 4. Many HW configurations can survive, but *all* must have MS-DOS | 3. The leading user of MS-DOS—i.e., IBM—will become the standard; "IBM-compatible" will be required |
| 1. IBM + DOS will be one of many; lots of other HW/OS configurations can fight and survive | 2. *One* combo of HW + operating system will dominate, and soon—Apple? IBM/DOS? Other? |

**Rate of PC adoption is slow** (left) **Rate of PC adoption is fast** (right)

**MS-DOS will be one of many**

How would you have used a grid like this? Would you have continued to bet only on quadrant 1, that your combination of proprietary box plus proprietary operating system could win? That's what many of the twenty-plus competitors at the time did, including then-giants Xerox, Digital Equipment (also known as DEC when it was alive), and Wang.

Would you have looked at this grid, said something along the lines of "Balls!," and then hedged your bets by also investing in peripherals, especially printers, because printers and other peripherals would be needed no matter whose boxes and whose operating systems won? That's what Hewlett-Packard did, and even twenty years later, it's the printers that are fueling HP's bottom line.

Would you have said, "Yep, IBM and DOS are going to pose a lot of danger to us in one way or another, so let's do what they do but better and cheaper," so you could survive or even do well no matter which of the four quadrants turned out to be the case (though you'd do best if the future looked more like quadrant 3)? That's what three engineers from Texas Instruments—Ron Canion, Jim Harris, and Bill Murto—did, starting a company called Compaq with the first real IBM-compatible and first portable PC (well, at twenty-eight pounds, the first "luggable").

Or, changing our initial rules for this example and now placing you at Apple, would you have stuck to your strategy of high prices and a closed system?

As computer-history buffs (and former Apple addicts) know, Apple chose the "if it ain't broke, don't fix it" strategy. And not without reason: in the early 1980s, Apple had a 50 percent market share, a proprietary and closed operating system that was worlds better than Microsoft's DOS product (first known as PC-DOS), better hardware, premium prices, and fanatically and fiercely loyal customers. *Nonetheless, once Gates unleashed his PC-DOS strategy, the landscape changed irretrievably and, for that reason, so did the criteria for wise bets.* And while HP and Compaq made bets that allowed them to reduce the risks of betting against future trends, Apple bet on quadrants 1 and 2 (with the Apple operating system as the winner) and therefore neither dropped its prices nor opened its operating system to applications developers.

Fast forward two decades, and HP had acquired Compaq and become the world market-share leader in PCs. Wang, DEC, and most of the other companies that had bet only on quadrant 1 were long since dead. Apple was the exception but only barely, with a share of the world market for PCs of just a few percent—and a new lease on life from Steve Job's latest invention, the iPod.

## Rethinking Existing Risks:
## Shopping Malls in the Mideast

It's easy to see better bets in hindsight, of course, because by then the uncertainties have been resolved and the Wild Cards are wild no longer. The intent of the Uncertainty Grid is to give you ways to manage these risks in real time, *before* you know the answer.

That was the issue facing a large multinational company that Eileen was working with and that was developing shopping malls in Middle Eastern countries in partnership with a well-connected and very wealthy family from the area. When a group of top managers from the Western company had an internal meeting at about the time the final agreements were to be signed, they came up with the following grid. (We've given the quadrants names to reflect how they seemed to the Western company.)

## Uncertainty Grid: Middle East Shopping Malls, 2000

Oil prices tumble

| | | |
|---|---|---|
| The big guy continues to love us | 4. Struggle Together | 3. Nightmare Land | The big guy falls out of love with us |
| | 1. Dreamland | 2. Sabotage City | |

Oil prices stay high

Eileen then broke the group into four subteams and assigned one quadrant per team, giving each the three-year question: "If I could tell you now, for certain, that in three years this will be the situation you will be in, what bets would you then wish that you had made now?"

It was about at this point that the meeting fell apart. The senior-most executive in the room stood up and objected strenuously on the grounds that the contracts were almost done and he was not going to stand for any second thoughts at this point in the proceedings. So Eileen proposed a deal: the group would spend fifteen minutes on the task and if after that he still thought the assignment was useless, they'd stop. At which point Eileen assigned him and his group to answer the question from the perspective of quadrant 3, Nightmare Land.

Fifteen minutes later, the group working on quadrant 3 wanted to make an immediate change—not in the agenda for the day, but in the company's strategy. The approach they wanted the company to move from, and the one to which it had already agreed, was division of the combined assets in proportion to the ownership shares in the case of disagreements or contractual disputes. The approach they wanted to move to was more along the lines of each side retaining control of the assets they brought to the deal—the real estate for the Middle Eastern family and the brands for the Western company. Not only would this mitigate the negative consequences of a quadrant-3 world for both sides, it also provided better protection or gave no harm if any of the other three quadrants pertained. In this situation, the search for risk splits gave both sides a way to shed and sidestep some of the Wild Card risks.

## AND A NOTE ON RATHOLE OPTIONS

In early 1993 it didn't really look like Microsoft got the Internet or would ever catch up, much to the delight of IBM, Sun, Oracle, and other big companies that saw the opportunity and were rushing to fill it. As Steve Ballmer, then the number-two guy at the company, told

one Microsoftie, J. Allard, who was agitating for at least some investment in the new technology, "I don't know what it is. I don't want to
know what it is. . . . Make it go away." About a year later, David
Marquardt, a Silicon Valley venture capitalist, bugged Bill Gates
along the same lines. "His [Gates's] view was the Internet was free,"
Marquardt later recalled. "There's no money to be made there. Why
is that an interesting business?"

In our framework, Gates and Ballmer would have put the Internet
in the Strategic Rat Hole Zone—a factor with very high uncertainty
but little likely future impact on their business. Enormous effort put
into these rat holes usually sucks up resources that would be more
profitably used on other bets. But that doesn't mean that no bets
should be placed on the Rat Hole factors because sometimes even the
best of us make incorrect assessments about the future impacts and
degrees of uncertainty. So, just in case, it can be worth placing a few
small side bets, in the event that your assessments were wrong. We
think of these as Rat Hole options.

In big companies, often these side bets are placed without top
management being fully aware of what's happening or why; these are
the "skunkworks" projects of the type that Peters and Waterman celebrated in their book on high-performing companies, *In Search of
Excellence*. In Microsoft's case, one of these was an unsanctioned
project that Allard launched in early 1993 to develop the company's
first Internet server that could link Microsoft to other Internet sites.
Other internal projects and converts followed, creating a growing
mass of knowledge and people that prodded Gates and Ballmer into
the Net—and, once in, gave Gates and Ballmer a base they could then
leverage to change the direction and future of the company in record
time.

Chance is good, and chance plus intent is even better. A small portion of your resources placed in small side bets on the Rat Hole factors may waste a little money or time, and most often they will. But
since once in a while they pay off big, small investments in a few Rat
Hole bets can be an important part of a prudent strategy.

\*     \*     \*     \*

Navigating uncertainty is a fact of life, in business and out. No one can eliminate risk entirely and many people pay far too much for the illusion of certainty. The inevitability of risk gives the smart gambler two options. One is to shift or redistribute the risks a little and over time improve aggregate returns a lot. The other is, in those cases where other people are willing to overpay for certainty, to take the other side of those bets and take on risks that hold disproportionate payoffs and up the aggregate returns that way too.

In both cases, you make your own luck when you understand that risk and return are not always perfectly balanced and then, in line with that realization, you find ways to either offload some of the risk and keep a healthy payoff, or live with the risk and increase the payoffs.

## THE UNMARKED DOORS

*You are faced with a terrible dilemma, the worst dilemma in your life. On the one hand, you have been told by sources you trust of an imminent and terrible situation. It could be an impending severe military threat to your country, or concerns that your niece is being abused by her stepfather, or evidence of a massive fraud being perpetrated inside your company. If the information is correct, you need to act quickly to avoid catastrophic consequences. On the other hand, you don't have all the facts and you also understand that what you've been told could be wrong. If you act on the basis of incorrect information, you could inadvertently make the situation far worse than if you had waited.*

*As you think about your situation, you realize that this is like the old story in which a prisoner has to open one of two doors, one of which hides a beautiful lady and the other, a hungry tiger. When you draw the map of your choices, outcomes, and consequences, you also see two doors. In your case, one door is marked "act" and the other is marked "don't act," and your map looks like this:*

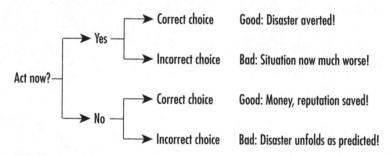

*What do you do—and why?*

*(Incidentally, if you took the political version of this problem, did you think of Laocoon and the Trojan Horse, George W. Bush and the war in Iraq in 2003, or Neville Chamberlain and the Munich Pact with Hitler in 1938?)*

## The Gambler's Dozen, Step 10

# POINT OF ACTION:
## Find the Core "It" of Your Bets

A SAD LIMERICK

The A-team of execs said, "Oh, screw it!

Get everyone going; just do it!"

But under the bubbles

Lurked boatloads of troubles

'Cuz the "it" was unclear—and none knew it!

# 10. Point of Action: What's the "It" I'm Betting On?

WE are now at the point of action. If you are ready to bet, do you know the "it" you are betting on?

When master golfers set up a shot, their answer to this question will be yes. A Tiger Woods may not know for certain whether he will hit the green or sink the putt, but you can be sure that he is very clear on three things: how he is going to play the ball; the specific outcome he is aiming to achieve; and the predictions he is making that tell him that this club, this stance, and this swing are more likely to get his ball close to the cup than some other approach.

As we diagrammed at the beginning of this book, we view these three aspects—intent, prediction, and action—as the core "it" of a bet. One might think that, at the point of action, most bettors would be able to describe the "it" of their bets roughly as well as a good golfer can. Our experience is that the reverse is true; that many people, even or perhaps most especially very smart people, tend to get caught in the same sad trap that our limerick friends got caught in and are unclear about the real "it" of the bets they are about to place.

Articulating the "it" of any betting plan—what you are going to do and why—is the tenth skill of Predictive Intelligence. This is a PA! skill, combining prediction and action, and it requires you to identify, with some specificity, the core content of the actions you are going to take, with the intent of creating what outcomes, based on what predictions about how action A will create or foster result B.

In some ways, this step is the one among the Gambler's Dozen that's the most fun because it's here that you put everything from the previous nine together to create your bets. It's also a critically important step. If you can outline the core "it" of your bets in terms of intent, prediction, and action, you can then see how these three pieces fit together and see what adjustments, if any, you will want to make before you act. It's also the step that can be toughest, because describing the "it" crisply and clearly is a deceptively difficult task.

One thing we've learned about this step is that the sequence for addressing the pieces of intent, prediction, and action doesn't matter as long as you cover all three and then check how well each fits the others. One way to address these three pieces, and perhaps the most logical, is to go from intent to predictions to action. In practice, we find that many people do better when we let them start with the action part and then work backwards to intent and underlying predictions, checking the links as they go. We think the reason for this is that people often build implicit commitment to a plan of action before they're fully aware of what they've decided to do and why. In these cases, starting where the mind is becomes the most efficient way of proceeding.

Whatever order you do the pieces in, we find it helps to be brief and clear, as though you were preparing a three-slide PowerPoint presentation for a boss or investor. And in fact, that's exactly the approach we recommend here, except that the boss or investor we want you to think about is one who is nearsighted, so you have to use a large font and only a limited number of words, and who is cranky about language, so you have to use words that are clear and that you can define (no "better quality" or "enhanced value" if you can't tangibly define what you mean by those nice phrases).

We also ask that you check the links between the three slides as you go. If you see critical disconnects between the core content of what you plan to do (the action), the outcomes you are trying to achieve (the intent), and the basis for your confidence about your ability to get where you want to go (the predictions), redo your bets and then change your slides to match the change in your plans.

So, if you're ready, here are some ideas to think about as you construct your three slides to describe the core "it" of your betting plan.

## SLIDE 1: ACTION—CONTENT OF THE "IT"

A Fortune 50 company is about to launch the new version of one of its premier products. When it comes time to do the market research to refine the pricing, it turns out that no one can describe, crisply and specifically, exactly what the customers will be getting and why or how these new benefits are superior to what the competition offers.

A leading teaching hospital is three months away from opening a ward with a new service model for the treatment of certain kinds of patients. There's substantial excitement, even though the specifics of exactly what will be different and how have yet to be worked out.

A high-tech company has poured millions into a new technology with all sorts of wonderful bells and whistles. When asked if the new product will come anywhere close to the basic requirements the company's target customers say are their "must haves," it becomes clear that the question has never been asked before and that the answers don't look promising.

These three examples reflect the same problem—smoke bombs that obscure the core content of the "it." We see a lot of business plans, and because we see a lot of business plans, we see a lot of smoke bombs. These smoke bombs are of a very particular sort; the subsidiary "its" are clear, but the core "it" is not. So we typically find a good amount of detail on the overall markets to be served, the technologies to be used, the financing strategies, and the sales and distribution plans. But what's not in at least half of these plans is even a fairly reasonable first draft of the content part of the "it"—what the substance of the new endeavor is, with what costs to the company and what relative advantages and disadvantages to the customers.

Consider Iridium, perhaps the poster child for companies that generate and then choke on their own smoke bombs. Iridium, founded by Motorola, is the wireless communications company we first mentioned in Chapter 3. Management at Iridium did an outstanding job of getting its sixty-six satellites (down from the original plan of seventy-seven) designed, manufactured, deployed, and functioning in their low-earth orbit (LEO) format in record time. And management also did an outstanding job of securing the financing for the venture, about $5 billion worth in total, from a combination of private equity, a very successful IPO, bonds, and bank loans.

What the managers at Iridium did not do well was to define the core "it" of their product. Had you asked Iridium management to construct their product "it" slide in 1998, when the company launched its commercial services, we imagine they would have used phrases like "Freedom to Communicate" and "with anyone, anytime, virtually anywhere in the world." We imagine this because these are the things they did say to the financial markets and also to their prospective customers in a $140 million global advertising campaign.

But had you asked us—and we had numerous conversations about Iridium in 1997 and '98—we would have said that Iridium's words about its "it" wouldn't pass our "cranky boss" test. They aren't specific, they aren't crisp, and, when you parse through them, they don't tell what you will actually get and what you will have to pay.

Here's what our "no-smoke" version of the core "it" of the Iridium product would have looked like:

## Iridium "It" Slide 1: Content of the "It," 1998

- Customer purchases Iridium service and also the phone
- Iridium service covers all parts of the globe, including places not covered today—ships and oil rigs at sea, remote locations
- Allows cross-border communications between countries with conflicting telecoms standards (e.g., between countries in Europe)
- Iridium phones need direct line-of-sight from phone to satellite; therefore often don't work in buildings, under trees, or in dense urban locations
- Can fit phone with special oversized antenna to help with this problem
- Base Iridium phone: 7" long (without antenna)
- Iridium phone weight: about 1 pound
- Price to purchase Iridium phone: $2200–$3400
- Usage fees, $2–$7 per minute (difficult to lower costs and therefore prices due to capacity constraints in the satellites)

It appears that at least to some extent, people inside Iridium knew that they were having problems cutting through their own smoke. As John Richardson, Iridium's last CEO, described to *Forbes* magazine in 1999 just prior to the company's bankruptcy filing, "The message about what this product was and where it was supposed to go changed from meeting to meeting. . . . One day we'd talk about cellular applications, the next day it was a satellite product. When we launched in November [1998], I'm not sure we had a clear idea of what we wanted to be. . . . We did all the really difficult stuff, like building the network and did all the no-brainer stuff at the end poorly."

Richardson was wrong in one respect. Defining the content of your core "it" is not no-brainer stuff and it's not something you do at the end. Otherwise you can wind up having spent $5 billion only to discover that, when all the smoke clears, you didn't know whether the content of your "it" could ever support the outcomes you wished to achieve.

## SLIDE 2: INTENT—WHAT OUTCOMES AND WHY

In the 1970s, in the Midlands of England, there was a bus route that ran from Bagnall to Greenfields. Passengers on this route weren't very happy, however, because the bus drivers routinely passed them by with a wave and a smile but without stopping. When complaints were registered, this was the response:

"It is impossible for the drivers to keep to their timetable if they have to stop for passengers."

All bets start with intent, as we diagrammed in the introduction and then discussed in Chapter 1. When you're at the point of action, and whether you are starting with the intent piece or are working backward from the action piece, you need to be able to articulate the specific outcomes you want to achieve and what these outcomes will do for you or allow you to do.

This can be tougher than one might initially think. At the Midlands bus company, for example, the outcome being sought was simple enough—adherence to the timetable. What's unclear is how management of the company had arrived at the conclusion that leaving passengers stranded by the side of the road was a better result than, say, revising its schedules to match the demand for its services.

Or think about building designs and advertising campaigns. It sometimes seems that the more famous the architects are, the more likely it is that the outcomes being sought are accolades from other architects rather than from the people who paid for their services or will use the buildings.

Advertising campaigns can fall into a similar confusion in intent, even for very successful and savvy companies. Consider Coke's 2004 "armpit" commercial spot, aired during a golf tournament.

The ad went like this: a sweaty guy breaks from a game of hoops. He grabs a cold can of Coke from the fridge, gulps it down, grabs a second one for his friend, which, before he hands it over, he uses to cool off by pressing it to his sweat-drenched forehead, neck, and stomach. Next, our hero, the sweat hog, lifts his arm and rubs the can under his bare armpit. Only then does he give it to his friend, who, having not seen the prior set of steps, pops the can and drinks from it.

Now remember, the venue we're talking about for this ad isn't MTV. The venue is a televised golf tournament, with just the kinds of viewers you'd expect for a televised golf tournament including, in this particular case, Donald Keough, a member of Coke's board of directors and a former president of the company.

Reportedly, like Queen Victoria, Keough was not amused. This probably mattered to Coke's number-two executive at the time, Steven Heyer, who was being considered for promotion to the number-one job at Coke, especially since the search committee that would decide whether he, or rival E. Nevill Isdell, would get the job was being headed by . . . Donald Keough. Heyer was a big proponent of the ad, which, sources said, he and others liked because it was "edgy." Though you may not be surprised that the job went to Isdell, you may wonder, as we do, what intent Heyer and those of his colleagues who agreed with him had in mind when they decided to air that ad during a golf tournament.

In Iridium's case, lack of clarity on the intent part of the "it" was not one of many problems the company had. Quite to the contrary, company insiders knew exactly what they wanted to achieve and why these outcomes would be of value. If we had asked Iridium's management to put together a clear and internally consistent slide on this subject, we suspect they could have done it in no time flat and that it might have looked something like this:

---

### Iridium "It" Slide 2: Intent

Outcomes we want to achieve:
- Sign on 50,000 customers per month in 1999 (600,000 in total)
- Even with slippage, sign on at least 400,000 customers in total by end of 1999

Value of these outcomes to us:
- Breakeven volume is 400,000 subscribers
- Loan covenants require us to have at least 52,000 subscribers by end of March 1999
- If we can hit at least 400,000 subscribers by end of 1999, we can go it alone or sell external sources on another round of financing

---

Now, say it's late 1998 or early 1999 and you own Iridium stock, which you bought at $20 per share at the IPO and which is now trading at almost $50 per share. Most of the analysts in the Wall Street houses have "buy" recommendations for the stock. An investment analyst at Salomon Smith Barney is forecasting that the stock will reach $60 per share soon. Do you sell, hold, or buy more?

## SLIDE 3: PREDICTIONS—FORECASTS AND CONFIDENCE LEVELS

Predictions are the connective tissue of any bet. At the point of action, it's important to be clear about the predictions that your bets will depend most on—and about how much confidence you have that events will transpire in a way you predict will be satisfactory to you.

There are innumerable ways to make predictive errors, and three primary ones. One is to make incorrect predictions about what will be satisfactory to you in the future, as we discussed in Chapters 1 and 2. That's an error you may have made if you get the person of your dreams to marry you and then, once into the marriage, you discover that "high maintenance" doesn't even begin to describe what you have to put up with every day. That's also the error you make if you get the job you've always hoped for and find that, while the kind of life you are now living may be great for some people, it isn't for you.

And that's the error that many entrepreneurs make when they seek weak or ineffective boards of directors. These entrepreneurs may get what they want: the ability to manage without interference, especially in their area of expertise of technology or science. But they also suffer when they discover that they've placed a bunch of poor business bets—about how to finance the company, for example, or where to put the primary product development and sales efforts—that could have been averted with the assistance of an able and enabled board. Of course, by then it's too late, for the entrepreneur, the investors, and the board.

A second kind of predictive error is to have a good outcome in mind, but to miss the intervening variables that will affect whether you achieve this result. That was the problem Kimberly-Clark encountered when it raised its prices, anticipating that P&G would follow so that both could enjoy an extra $50 million or more on their respective bottom lines. K-C's prediction about the relationship between the action of raising prices, and the desired result of boosting the bottom line, was correct, but the company missed the fact that other variables can intervene between the action and desired result, as we discussed in Chapter 2 and then again in Chapter 8.

The third error is to miss the direct connection between action A and result B, even without wild cards like P&G. That's the mistake that Iridium made, and this mistake was evident at the time to anyone who compared Iridium's predictions about the numbers and desires of its prospective customers to what the company was actually offering and what these prospective customers could get elsewhere—what we think of as the "good deal" test, your product benefits at your price versus your competitors' product benefits at their prices.

It may be that Iridium had made its predictions earlier in the company's history and hadn't tracked changes in the industry since then. Still, it's useful when you're betting based on prior predictions, to look at what you thought would happen, and then scan the environment for evidence of whether the world has been moving in the direction you had forecasted. If management at Iridium had done this, they might have sped up their efforts to create a viable Plan B.

Here's our "it" slide of Iridium's predictions versus what was actually happening in late 1998 and early 1999:

## Iridium "It" Slide 3: Predictions

Core predictions, satellite-based mobile phones:
- Satellites will be best way to provide worldwide wireless service
- People in business, military need cross-border coverage
- Iridium is the best satellite-based system
- Our service competes with outrageous hotel charges or no service at all
- Future satellite phone market: 12 million users by 2002 and growing
- 400,000 users in 1999 viable since 400,000 is small percentage of total market

Environmental scan, ground-based vs. satellite-based mobile phones:
- Ground-based mobile coverage growing fast everywhere
- Cross-border problem diminishing; GSM rapidly becoming single European standard, 150 million subscribers by early 1999, still growing
- Ground-based mobiles work indoors and in dense urban areas; ours don't
- Much cheaper usage fees for local calls (e.g., 9–11¢ per minute within U.S.) and for international calls to/from most locations
- Competition has much smaller and less costly handsets— Motorola's StarTac® introduced in 1998 at 4 inches long, 3 ounces, $600 before discounts
- Other mobiles a bit bigger than StarTac; all still much less expensive and much, much smaller and lighter than the Iridium handset

In other words, if you were stuck on an oil rig in the middle of the ocean somewhere or were in the outback of Australia, Iridium was the service for you. Otherwise, all Iridium offered to you was the opportunity to pay a lot more than the ground-based mobile companies were charging for the privilege of owning an oversized and overweight handset that wouldn't work in most urban areas.

Our answer to the sell, hold, or buy question? Sell, of course. As in the limerick that started this chapter, "Under the bubbles/lurked boatload of troubles/'cuz the 'it' was unclear—and none knew it!"

Although in the case of Iridium, eventually everyone did, because by May 1999 the company had only ten thousand subscribers (versus the two hundred thousand the company had forecasted), and by August 1999 it had defaulted on its debt and filed for bankruptcy protection. After $5 billion in investment, the company's assets were purchased for $25 million by a consortium of investors that included Edward F. Staiano, who had been Iridium's CEO from 1996 until his resignation from that post in April 1999.

*     *     *     *

At the core of every bet is the "it"—the content of what you plan to do, the outcomes you are trying to achieve, and the predictions on which you base your confidence that you will get where you will want to be. One way to think about the "it" is using the analogy of Saturn and Saturn's rings. The core "it" is like Saturn itself. The rings are the secondary and tertiary differentiators and details—all the stuff that orbits around and depends on the core "it" to be valuable.

When you can articulate the core "it" you're betting on and have checked the links between the pieces, you've upped your odds of getting where you want to go. And when you can understand the "it" that others are betting on, you've increased your own ability to assess those situations that you want to join in or stay involved with . . . and those that you might prefer to avoid or deflect.

Many companies and many people are precise about the secondary and tertiary issues and vague about the core "it." This is a losing strategy. Bets with great detail on the secondary and tertiary level issues will fail if the core "it" is not in place. If you want to make your own luck, be clear about the core "it" first; then, if that "it" looks solid, fill in the details about the secondary issues and differentiators. And if the core "it" doesn't look solid, stop and either fix the "it" or walk away. Otherwise you will be just adding embroidery to a bad-luck magnet.

# THE RADIANT BRIDE

*You go to a wedding. As with many weddings you have attended, and perhaps even your own, you notice that while the bride looks lovely and is wearing a beautiful gown, the bridesmaids don't look quite as lovely. And then you notice that their dresses, which the bride selected and the bridesmaids had to pay for, are—not to put too fine a point on it— kind of ugly.*

*You know that this isn't always true, but you've now seen it enough that you begin to wonder why the bridesmaids always seem to be decked out in rather hideous dresses.*

*The question for this puzzle is: why?*

*Here's a worksheet to get you started on your answer:*

- *Action:*


- *Intent:*


- *Underlying Predictions:*



*(And if you doubt that bridesmaids' dresses are often ugly, go to www.uglydress.com, or see how many hits you get if you do a Web search on "ugly bridesmaid dresses," or check out "Attack of the Ugly Bridesmaid Dresses," at http:// home.earthlink.net/lsontag/page12.htm.)*

**The Gambler's Dozen, Step 11**

# DOMINO EFFECTS:
Assess the Required
Follow-on Bets

# Green Ears and Ham

WHEN children hit the two-to-three–year age range, they start telling little fibs. That's part of the natural development of kids. And helping kids learn to take responsibility for what they say and do is part of the job of the parent.

When Howard's son Willie was about two and a half years old, he began telling little stories, just as other kids do at that age. Howard wanted to help Willie get a sense that other people could tell if he was straying from the truth, but he wanted to do so gently. So one day when Willie came in with another little story, Howard said, "Willie, I don't think what you're telling me is quite the truth."

"How do you know?" said Willie.

"Well," said Howard, "when you don't tell the truth, your ears turn green."

The next time Willie came in to tell his father a fib, he had his hands over his ears.

# 11. Domino Effects:
# Will I Be Locked into a Tight Set of
# Follow-on Bets?

MOST objectives require a sequence of bets: you make an initial bet and then at intervals make follow-on bets. In many situations, you have multiple options at each subsequent decision point, some that you anticipated when you placed the initial bet and others that emerged as you went along. If you've decided to go to Florence on holiday, you know that while your options for entertaining yourself there aren't limitless, they are almost so, and that if you really tire of fabulous food, art, music, shopping, and strolling, you can hop on a train and go hiking in the countryside, sailing in the Adriatic, or decamp to another country entirely.

Some bets, though, are more like the first domino pushed in a domino-toppling contest; once you make the first move, you've set off a chain reaction that locks you into a tight range of options for your next steps. If you've decided to conquer Everest or go white-water rafting on the Colorado River, once you're moving up the mountain or down the river, your options for tomorrow are pretty well set. That was also the case for Willie Stevenson when he decided to try another fib on his dad; by toddler logic, if he didn't want to tell the truth, the follow-on bet was that he also had to do something about his ears.

The eleventh skill of the Gambler's Dozen, and the one this step is based on, is to understand the type and range of follow-on bets you may be signing up for, before you topple the first domino. This is a PA!—Predict and Act!—skill. It requires you to assess whether the bet you are about to make will start a chain reaction of follow-on bets and, if so, whether you are prepared to live with this limited set of options.

Two quick tests can help you see if your initial bet is going to entail a fairly narrow range of follow-on bets. The first is to ask whether the bet you are about to take involves a known and consistent sequence of steps. If so, the follow-on bets required to stay in the game are known too. We call these the "built-in bets" and they comprise the predetermined path you will have to follow for as long as you want to stay in this game.

When you step into the raft on the first day of a seven-day whitewater wilderness trip or initiate a lawsuit against a company that is infringing your patent, you're in the "built-in" territory. You may or may not know this the first time you go rafting or file a lawsuit, but you surely do the second time.

If the first test is negative, your options may still be limited due to the reaction by other people to what you are trying to achieve. To test for this, we go to a second question and ask whether significant resistance can be expected to the results being aimed for. We ask this because in these situations, the stronger the expected resistance, the more you can also anticipate, even before your first move, that you will be faced with a limited menu of follow-on bets that you will have to take to get where you want to go. We call these the "bolt-on bets" and they typically lock you into a narrow range of options for follow-on bets to counter the resistance, unless you decide to modify your goals or opt out of the situation entirely.

Sometimes these bolt-on bets lead to better and more creative solutions, just as community resistance to a new building or real estate development often inspires better architectural designs. And sometimes these bolt-on bets lead to worse and worse solutions, as Willie Stevenson discovered in a small way at age two and a half—and as the grown-up executives involved in the accounting frauds at Enron, Royal Dutch/Shell Group, Parmalat, and WorldCom demonstrated in a more massive way in the 1990s and into the new century.

The issue with both the built-ins and the bolt-ons is not that they are always bad, but that the sooner you can see them, the sooner you can decide if your current objectives are going to be worth the kinds of follow-on bets you now see that you will have to take.

Or, of course, you can keep your hands over your ears.

## CHECK 1: BUILT-IN DOMINO EFFECTS

If you have ever been involved with a young company that wants to get a new medicine to the market, you know about objectives that lead to built-in domino effects. First, you know that if you want to market your drug in the United States, you will have to go through the FDA approval process. Second, you know that you will have to raise multiple rounds of funding and you know approximately how much you'll need to raise. And third, you know the kinds of milestones you'll have to hit to raise each of those rounds on attractive terms. Even though you don't know whether you will be able to hit the milestones, you do know that once you establish your enterprise, you have simultaneously signed up for a known sequence of bets.

So say you are the chairman of a company that has a new therapeutic agent for some terrible disease that currently has few good treatment options, AIDS, for example, or pancreatic cancer. Your company has completed all its discovery and preclinical testing, and is just about through its Phase 1 drug trial, focusing on the safety of the compound in humans. You and all the scientists are thrilled with the results from the Phase 1 study not only because the results exceeded what you had hoped for in terms of safety, but also because the data showed early evidence of effectiveness.

The phone rings. On the other end is one of the top people from a leading pharmaceutical company. With your permission, a member of your board has shared some of the information about your new compound with this other company. After a few pleasantries, the caller outlines a deal in which his company would buy a big chunk of your company. All things considered, the terms are pretty nice. Current investors would get some cash now and would keep some equity in the venture going forward. The valuation used for the proposed transaction is attractive for a company at this stage in its development, but obviously is not anywhere close to what the company would be worth after completion of a successful Phase 2.

You know that your company will have the same sequence of follow-on bets, regardless of whether you do this deal or stay independent, which is to go through the Phase 2 trials and then Phase 3 trials to test effectiveness and further test safety and dosage. Both trials will require many more patients than the Phase 1 study, and a lot of time, maybe two years for Phase 2 and three to four years for Phase 3. Then you will need to file an NDA (New Drug Application), which will likely take another year and a half. You figure that you will need to raise at least $100 million more in total to get through all these steps. You have also been told, based on past experience of similar compounds, that the odds of your drug making it through this whole process are something on the order of one in three to one in four.

What do you do: take the deal and reduce the downside, or preserve the upside and tell the exec that you'll get back to him toward the end of the Phase 2 trials? Which alternative would you choose if you were an investor in this company? What about if you were the founder-scientist, and your dream was to end the scourge of AIDS or the death sentence of a pancreatic cancer diagnosis? What if you were the founder-scientist, and your real objective was to win the Nobel Prize?

Answering these questions well requires that you understand both the built-in follow-on bets you will be required to take plus your own situation as reflected in the first four steps of the Gambler's Dozen— step 1 on the Big Goals especially, and also step 2 on Upside/Downside, step 3 on Jump Bets, and step 4 on Campaign Plans. If your primary goal is to get the compound into humans as soon as possible and make some money for sure but not necessarily to max out your potential return, you might be inclined to trying to work out a deal with a big partner now. If your primary goal is to make a huge score from this investment with a much bigger risk of losing everything, you may be more interested in getting through Phase 2 and then talking with potential industry partners.

## CHECK 2: BOLT-ON DOMINO EFFECTS

A symphony orchestra with a stodgy subscriber base believes that its customers should be exposed to contemporary classical music as part of the orchestra's regular programming. A manufacturing company with skyrocketing healthcare costs believes that its employees should take more responsibility for their healthcare decisions and bear more of the costs. A university town with rising housing costs believes that its low-income and elderly citizens should not be priced out of the rental market and forced to move.

The operative word in these three situations is *should*. But "shoulds" are tricky. Even when the goals are worthy, other parties often have strongly held views based on different "shoulds" or desires. Then, using our second test for domino effects, you can be fairly certain that these people will resist what you're trying to do, probably quite vigorously, and also that in consequence you'll have to follow your original bet with a fairly narrow range of bolt-on bets to counter the resistance. In these kinds of situations, the earlier you can see the kinds of bolt-on bets you're signing up for, the faster you can figure out whether you can live with them or whether you want to change or reframe your objectives.

One factor to look at when you're trying to understand whether you will be locked into a fairly narrow range of bolt-on bets is your power relative to that of the people who don't like your objectives. A rich and famous symphony orchestra serving a large and deep market of classical music lovers—Boston, for example, or Paris, or Chicago, or Amsterdam—may be able to sandwich a new piece of discordant music by an unknown composer in a program that starts with Brahms and ends with Beethoven, and survive with only a small loss in subscriptions and donations. A small and struggling orchestra may not, but might be able to consider some "new music" special concerts, outside the normal subscription series.

In the same way, companies with good labor pools and weak unions can shift some of the healthcare cost burden to their employees as a kind of take-it-or-leave-it proposition. Those with either labor shortages or strong unions quickly find that such a frontal approach leads to disaster and may instead opt for a consumer-driven health plan option that allows employees to set up some form of a health savings account while also involving higher co-pays on certain services.

Or consider the matter of a university town with rising housing costs. We'll take Cambridge, Massachusetts, as our case study, starting in the 1960s when the mix of radical politics and rising housing prices created demand for some form of rent control. The result was Cambridge's 1970 rent-control law that froze rents at the then current levels and allowed increases only with the approval of a newly formed rent-control board.

Low-income people who lived in Cambridge benefited from rent control, as planned, but so did lots of young professionals who were making good money and knew how to work the system to lock in below-market rents; some estimates suggested that only 10 percent of the protected units in Cambridge were occupied by low-income or elderly tenants. Not surprisingly, landlords hated the law. They also had the power to resist, which they exercised by taking their units, on which they could now make little or no profit, converting them into condominiums, and then selling them. That gave the landlords two wins: first, they made a substantial one-time profit, and second, they got rid of an asset that would otherwise be an unprofitable headache.

The landlords' resistance led to Cambridge's bolt-on bet, and actually a rather ingenious one in a Catch-22 kind of way, to protect rent control. In 1979, the Cambridge City Council passed a law, the Removal Permit Ordinance, that simply prevented anyone who owned a condominium from living in it. Here's how it worked: the ordinance mandated that no residence could be removed from the rental stock of Cambridge unless the removal benefited "the persons sought to be protected" by the original rent control law. In other words, if you bought a residence in 1990 that had been rented out under rent control at some previous time in its history after 1979, you couldn't live in it. You could only rent it out—and only at rent-controlled rents. This then led to many of the remaining landlords neglecting their buildings and growing public pressure to overturn all of rent control, which finally occurred through a statewide vote in 1994.

If the Cambridge rent-control example seems too parochial, consider the experiments in Germany and France to limit work weeks to thirty-five hours per week with forty hours' pay, done through laws and labor agreements. The reasoning was that the regulations would lead to higher employment because the employers would require more workers working thirty-five hours a week to achieve the same results previously accomplished by a smaller number of workers putting in forty hours per week.

As with Cambridge rent control, the goal may have been admirable. But also like Cambridge rent control, the affected businesses had the power to resist, starting with their decisions about where to place new operations or make additional hires. (Moves back to a forty-hour work week were well underway in both countries by 2004. The employers' access to alternative labor options in the ten new members of the European Union may have been part of the reason.)

Sometimes, though, the power of a counter-party to resist a bet and force a set of unpleasant bolt-on bets isn't so obvious, especially if the resistor is small, and the people or entities making the initial bet assume that they, the big guys, have the power simply because they are larger, or more established, or wealthier.

That may be what led billion-dollar safety-products company Walter Kidde to ignore the claims of a small start-up, X-IT. What was clear in the case was that X-IT invented a new design for a home fire-escape ladder on which X-IT had a pending patent, that Kidde executives had met with X-IT executives, that Kidde made an offer to buy X-IT for $600,000 plus a small royalty per ladder, and that X-IT turned down this offer as too low.

Oh, and also that soon thereafter, Kidde began marketing a ladder almost identical to X-IT's in similar packaging, including the same picture as X-IT had used—a photograph of the sister-in-law and nephew of the inventor of X-IT's ladder using the X-IT ladder.

Perhaps executives at Kidde had assumed that Kidde had done nothing wrong, and that even if it had, a tiny and as yet unprofitable start-up with sales of maybe $300,000 per year was in no position to pursue legal recourse. And that might have been correct if X-IT's investor group hadn't included Howard and a few other outraged investors who raised a "fighting fund" for the company, and also if X-IT hadn't found very smart attorneys who were willing to take the case on a contingency basis.

X-IT sued Kidde for copyright infringement, misappropriation of trade secrets, and six other counts of business misconduct, starting an arduous two-year legal battle. On August 17, 2001, the jury came back with its verdict in favor of X-IT, and the award: $116 million in total, $21 million in compensatory damages and $95 million in punitive damages. The award was subsequently reduced to about $20 million for X-IT, but still a nice sum, especially considering that X-IT would have accepted a $3 million offer for the purchase of the company when it first began negotiating with Kidde.

Kidde made a set of bolt-on bets after it had looked at X-IT's product and the intellectual property behind it and then made a very low offer to acquire the company. We can't speculate on the intent but only on the outcome; sometimes the little guys have a lot more fighting power than might first appear. And that can make all the difference in the range of follow-on bets that a big guy might have to take.

\*   \*   \*   \*

Some bets come with reasonably predictable follow-on bets. If you aren't prepared to live with these follow-on bets, you will waste your 100 marbles by even taking the first bet. In these cases, you will almost always find that you can make more luck by changing your goals—or finding a different betting approach for achieving them.

# VOICE OF EXPERIENCE

*An experienced and highly successful corporate executive is listening to the tale of a failing start-up and its CEO who, no matter how many times he misses his numbers, keeps persisting with exactly the same approach because he is sure, as he loudly and repetitively insists, that he has the correct business model.*

*Finally the experienced exec looks up and comments, "This is what we always say in Alcoholics Anonymous. We say that an alcoholic is a person who conducts the same bottle-based experiment ten times with the same disastrous results each time, and then conducts it the eleventh time in the expectation and belief that this time the results will be different."*

*Many of us get stuck from time to time in bad domino-effects bets that we take repeatedly in the expectation and belief that "this time" the results will be different. Sometimes we do this in our personal lives, sometimes in our careers and the performance of our jobs, and sometimes in the way we run our organizations.*

*What are your domino bets? And are you willing to break the pattern of follow-on bets that you keep signing up for?*

# The Gambler's Dozen, Step 12

# GAME OVER:
# Know When to Call It Quits

# All You Can Eat

YOU are invited to a buffet. When you get there, you discover the most wonderful array of foods and wines. Caviar and cheese of the highest quality, lobster and beef tenderloin expertly prepared, the most beautiful fruits and vegetables you have ever seen, gorgeous desserts, all selected and presented by some of the world's best chefs.

Your hosts are gracious, and invite you to eat and drink to your heart's content and to stay as long as you wish.

There are only two constraints. You can't take any of the food away with you in a doggie bag, and once you leave, you can't come back.

When do you call it quits?

# 12. Game Over: How Will I Know When to Call It Quits?

EVERY bet—large or small, corporate or personal—puts you into a game. And whatever the game, at some point your participation ends. Sometimes it ends because the game is over for all the players, sometimes because your participation is terminated by others, and sometimes because you've chosen to exit the game.

Once you've placed the bet, though, you always have to choose one of three broad options, which we'll call Option A, Option B, and Option C. Option A is to stay in the game as an active player until some later time or until someone or something boots you out. Option B is to quit this game and then enter another game that will allow you to go after the same kinds of results you've been aiming for in the current game. And Option C is to quit this game and go to a different kind of game that produces a different type of results.

If you invested $10,000 in Microsoft in March 1986 and have held onto it since, or held on and added to your stake, you were making Option A–type choices. If you made the same investment in Microsoft at the same time but sold your stake in December 1999 and then reinvested your $6 million or so of proceeds into other publicly traded equities or into a venture fund, you made an Option B choice at the time of the sale. And if you sold your stake in December 1999 and then sailed around the world or began work on a series of nonprofit ventures, you made an Option C choice at the time you sold your stock.

The final skill of the Gambler's Dozen, and the one this step is based on, is figuring out how you will know when to go for Options B or C and call it quits on the current game. To do this, we first assess what our best option seems to be based on: our satisfaction to date with the current game, our predictions about future results, and our intent going forward. And then we go back for another heart check, just as we did in step 1, the Big Goals, to make sure that we don't have hidden emotion loops pulling us toward an option that is less likely to help us reach the goals we say we want to achieve.

## ESTIMATE FORWARD TO ASSESS WHETHER TO STAY OR QUIT

When we think about whether we want to stay and play, quit and play again, or quit and start a different kind of game, we try to figure out three things: current satisfaction, prediction about next results of staying in the current game, and our going-forward intent. Then we combine these three into a simple "estimator" that we use to assess which of the options—A, B, or C—looks like the best for us.

The most minimal form of this "estimator" uses only two alternatives for each of the three variables, and that's the one we show here. Though obviously you can make these assessments more complex and add more classifications, we limit the first run-through to just two alternatives per dimension which then generate eight distinct profiles that we can use to help us assess what we want to do. Even if you prefer more shades of gray, we recommend that you try it the simple way before you add more alternatives. (The math behind this is that two alternatives for three dimensions gives $2^3$ or 8 profiles. Three alternatives for three dimensions gives $3^3$ or 27 profiles.)

Satisfaction is the first dimension we look at, focusing on *how satisfied we are with the results to date* of the current game. We define the results to date in terms of the desired currency of the return for whatever kind of bet we are looking at—money for investments, for example; love and support for marriages; money, challenge, and new opportunities for jobs. Then we assess our satisfaction as "high" or "low," with "high" being anything from pretty satisfied to very satisfied and "low" being anything from deeply unsatisfied to marginally satisfied.

Prediction is the second dimension we look at, and here we concentrate *on our prediction of the results we are likely to get* if we stick with Option A and stay in the current game as active players. We use the same definition for the currency of the future results as we did with the Satisfaction dimension, and again we use a very simple measure with only two alternatives. One alternative is that when we think about the future upside, future downside, and future rules and rulemasters, we predict that we have more to gain than to lose by staying in the game. The other is that we predict that we have more to lose than to gain.

Intent is the third dimension and for this one we ask *what kinds of results we want to achieve* in the next round—more of the same, or more of other kinds of results. An investor may say that she wishes to continue to build her financial assets, so she would check the column for "want more of the same kind." An executive who is looking at whether to divest a recent acquisition or buy other assets to build this business area would check the same column. The law partner who is thinking about retirement from a lucrative law practice and who really wants to go into teaching and shape minds or become a missionary and save souls would check the last column, "want other things."

When you put these three dimensions together, you get a simple matrix that looks like this. We've included a line for you to add your rationale or thinking for the initial ratings you make on each of the three dimensions:

## Time-to-Quit/Time-to-Stay Matrix

| SATISFACTION with results to date | | PREDICTION about results of next round | | INTENT for next round/ kind of results | |
|---|---|---|---|---|---|
| High | Low | More to gain than to lose | More to lose than to gain | Want more of same kind | Want other things |
| Rationale: | | Rationale: | | Rationale: | |

To use this matrix, take a bet you are currently in, and make your assessments on each of the three dimensions. Then match your profile to one of the eight on the following Time-to-Quit/Time-to-Stay Estimator. The last column on the Estimator tells you which of the three options—A, B, or C—fits this profile the best.

## The Gambler's Dozen
## Time-to-Quit/Time-to-Stay Estimator

| Profile | SATISFACTION with results to date | | PREDICTION about results of next round, same game | | INTENT for next round/kind of result now desired | | A? B? C? |
|---|---|---|---|---|---|---|---|
| | High | Low | More to gain than to lose | More to lose than to gain | Want more of same kind | Want other things | |
| 1 | X | | X | | X | | A |
| 2 | | X | X | | X | | A |
| 3 | X | | | X | X | | B |
| 4 | | X | | X | X | | B |
| 5 | | X | | X | | X | C |
| 6 | X | | | X | | X | C |
| 7 | | X | X | | | X | C |
| 8 | X | | X | | | X | C |

This matrix doesn't tell you the answer, but it will give you a roughly correct estimate of which option is likely the best for you if your initial assessments in the dimensions of satisfaction, prediction, and intent were also roughly correct.

So, say you're an investor in a start-up, and so far you've been somewhat disappointed in the performance of the company. You think the technology is solid but the management team, and particularly the CEO, isn't very strong. The board has begun to take a more active role, the founder-CEO has been made the Chief Science Officer, and a terrific new management team has been brought in. You are now seeing budgets and deadlines being hit, and customer feedback is more enthusiastic. The kinds of results you want—financial returns—haven't changed. The next round of financing is coming up and you have been asked if you want to participate.

This situation fits profile 2. If you are feeling pretty good about your predictions, your best option would be A, to stay in the game as an active investor. If this round is a down round, which means that your prior investment has now been substantially diluted and re-upping for this round would be the only way to see a real return on your investment, you will want to think hard about your predictions (and see who else is reinvesting this time around). If you still feel you put your X in the correct column, you are still in an Option A situation. A marriage that's gone through a rocky stage but now is beginning to work much better would fit this same profile.

Now say you are a top executive of IBM or AT&T in the late 1990s. IBM has been famous in the minds of consumers for its hardware, from the big 360s of the 1960s to its PCs of the 1980s, and all the storage media, including the hard disk drives, that go into its machines. Similarly AT&T has been almost synonymous with long-distance services to consumers. Both businesses have historically been great cash generators for the companies. Still, as you look forward, you see only mediocre returns or losses.

This situation is a good match for profile 3, and it's a common one for companies whose former core products are no longer the stars they once were. In both cases, your best option is B, to get out of this game—in these instances by divesting the businesses—and then enter another game where you think you can make more money. That's what IBM did in 2002 when it sold its HDD (hard disk drive) business to Hitachi and continued to build its position in consulting, where it had better odds of earning the kinds of returns it wanted. And that's also the point that AT&T got to in 2004, prior to its acquisition by SBC, when it finally decided to reduce its position in wireline residential services and focus on its commercial and business markets. People who decide to leave their spouses or change jobs often also have this same profile and similarly make an Option B decision.

Finally, let's go back to the buffet that started this chapter. Do you eat and drink as you normally would? Or do you splurge and consume a bit more? Or do you eat and drink until you feel like you could burst? Do you stay for one meal, or eat and then hang out for a while and then eat some more?

Or, to put the buffet example into a business context, say you're a senior executive, age sixty-something plus or minus, who has loved being at the top. You know that if you retire, you will never again have a position like this one in terms of financial compensation and business power. What do you do? When do you decide that you've had enough and are ready for playing a new type of game in which you can achieve different kinds of results?

For people who are ready to move on despite the pleasures of the table or the satisfactions of the job, these examples correspond to profile 8. In these cases, the most appropriate option is C, to quit this game and go to a different kind of game that produces results of a different type—if you are pretty certain that you're ready to change the intent of your bets, or at least that you are ready to modify or expand the kinds of results you are seeking. Businesses also face situations where Option C is the most appropriate option when they look at their financial returns and decide to share some of the wealth with their employees or their communities.

That's what John Tu and David Sun did when they sold 80 percent of their company, Kingston Technologies, to Softbank, the Japanese venture capital giant, in 1996 for $1.5 billion and then gave $100 million of their proceeds back to their employees. More typically, that's what fabulously successful entrepreneurs like Andrew Carnegie in the late 1800s or Bill Gates in the late 1900s do when they begin giving away big chunks of the wealth they have amassed. And it's what all of us do when we make major changes in our work and our lives.

Of course, the recommended options for each of the three profiles we just looked at share one big caveat—you need to check your emotions as well as your analysis. And the need to check your emotions brings us to the second review for figuring out when to call it quits on one bet and start another.

## LOOK INTO YOUR HEART TO CHECK THE PULL FROM THE PAST

If you look back at the Time-to-Quit/Time-to-Stay Estimator, you will note an interesting fact: in an analytic world, you really don't need the column that shows your satisfaction with the results to date. That's because the option suggested by the Estimator is based on your predictions and intent *for the future*, not the past.

So you might be wondering why we included the first dimension, satisfaction with results to date, in the Estimator at all.

The answer lies in the human heart. When we bet, many of us often look back rather than forward. One way we do this is when we're winning. Then, sometimes regardless of the predictions we have made about the likely results of the next round of the same game and our assessments of what we would like to achieve, we stay in the game. Gamblers do this in casinos when they think they're hot or on a streak. Lots of us do this when we stay in jobs or careers where we are doing well—getting promoted, making lots of money—but in our heart of hearts we're not very happy or feel we're badly shortchanging the other parts of our lives we care about.

The other way is when we're losing. Then, again regardless of our predictions and the intents we say are important to us now, we redouble our efforts for the current game, and sometimes our bets, to get back to even, and perhaps prove that we aren't losers. This is stubborn behavior, driven by emotion, and to the extent that either you predict that you have more to lose than to gain by staying in the game or that you now wish to achieve different kinds of results than this bet will provide you, it is losing behavior.

We've each made both these kinds of mistakes, and you may have as well. If you look at the action suggested by the Estimator and your gut says no, stop and look at your assessment in the Satisfaction column. Then ask yourself, is your past driving your ability to make the best choices in the last step in the Gambler's Dozen, determining when it's time to call it quits on this bet and start another one?

*    *    *    *

Every bet—large or small, corporate or personal—puts you into a game. And whatever the game, at some point your participation ends. The question is, do you control the exit because you've decided you've had enough and you're ready to go on to the next game, or does someone else?

# GREAT-UNCLE GRISWOLD

*Your great-uncle Griswold has just died. Not that you particularly liked the old buzzard, but your mom asked you to go to the funeral and then to the reading of the will, and so you went.*

*It turns out that Great-Uncle Griswold was very wealthy, much wealthier than you ever imagined. As you listen to the will, you also begin to wonder if that demented genie you've heard so much about hadn't also visited your great-uncle.*

*Because this is what the will stipulated:*

*You are to get $10 million from the estate at the age of seventy-three if you fulfill the following criteria: You have to work until then at a division of Great-Uncle Griswold's company, and this division, you also discover, happens to be located near your town. The job you will have to work at isn't very interesting but would be relatively simple for you to do, though you will have to show up every day and perform the tasks. You will get your current salary this year, and every year thereafter you will get the same compensation plus an increase pegged at the rate of inflation.*

*That's option 1. It turns out there's a second option, that goes like this:*

*If you are willing to move to your great-uncle's home town of Podunk, North Dakota, and work at an equally boring job, you get $20 million at age seventy-three.*

*Or, if you turn the two previous options down, you get $250,000 today.*

*Which option do you choose?*

- *Option 1: take the hometown job, retire at age seventy-three, and collect $10 million.*
- *Option 2: take the job in Podunk North Dakota, retire at age seventy-three, and collect $20 million.*
- *Option 3: decline both jobs and collect $250,000 today.*

*Write your answer here:* _____

# Conclusion:
## Make Your Own Luck

# The General Dilemma:
# You Bet Your Life (and Your Company)

WE began this book with an invitation, a quiz, and the General's Dilemma—George B. McClellan's choices at Antietam. We end with some thoughts on the General Dilemma, a quiz, and a few final words.

The General Dilemma is that all of us are always acting in the face of uncertainty, so every action is a bet, whether we act as we always have or as we had planned or whether we act in some new way and change course.

The specific dilemma is that each of us has to choose, this bet and not this one, and we have to choose all the time and in all areas of our lives.

And that's the rub. Everyone has to bet, but not everyone is equally good at figuring out *which* bets to place to get the results they will desire at the time the outcomes occur.

The difference is Predictive Intelligence, the ability to act in the face of uncertainty to bring about the results you desire. The higher your Predictive Intelligence, the more you are able to make your own luck.

The good news is that Predictive Intelligence is a bundle of skills that, like any other bundle of skills, can be built and improved. That's where the Gambler's Dozen comes in and that's what we've focused on in this book.

So, now that you've gone through our thinking on these twelve steps, are you up for a final quiz? We've composed this one of a few more puzzles based on themes that run through the Gambler's Dozen, followed by the answer sheet. As with the other puzzles in this book, it helps to write down your answers.

And with that, here is our final set of puzzles:.

# THE "MAKE YOUR OWN LUCK" QUIZ

1. An up-and-coming NFL quarterback and an up-and-coming McKinsey & Company consultant are seen as superstars by their employers.

Which one has higher Predictive Intelligence in their respective fields of football for the quarterback and business for the consultant?

___ a.) The quarterback
___ b.) The consultant
___ c.) The two are just about equal in Predictive Intelligence in their respective fields.

Rationale for your answer: _____

_____

2. Your demented genie reappears and invites you to reconsider the situation you were left in at the end of step 1, the Big Goals. In that situation, as you may recall, you got $10 million and the Lasker Prize, but your adversary and most bitter rival got $20 million and the Nobel Prize. Now the demented genie is giving you the option to ditch the original deal for a new one. In the new deal, you would get $5 million and your rival would get no money and neither of you would get either of the prizes. Do you take the new deal or stick with the old one?

We understand that this is a totally personal decision. Still, we'd like you to answer for you, given your own situation—would you take the new deal or stick with the old one?

___ a.) Take the new deal ($5 million for you, nothing for your rival)
___ b.) Keep the old deal ($10 million and the Lasker Prize for you, $20 million and the Nobel Prize for your rival)

3. You are about to do a major piece of market research on your lead product. The consultant you are working with on this piece of research wants all of you—you, your boss, and your eight direct reports—to put your predictions down on paper about what you each think the research will show. You are personally very confident that the research will show a set of important growth opportunities. You also know that you have one or two nay-sayers on your staff. While you've been working hard with these two to get them to act more like team players, you also feel that it's possible that one or both of them are thinking differently than you are.

Do you take the consultant's recommendation that you and the members of your staff write down your predictions? Why or why not?

___ a.) Yes

___ b.) No

Rationale for your answer: _____

_____

4. You and your sweetheart are about to get married. Your mother and your prospective mother-in-law and father-in-law all want a very big and elaborate wedding, though they aren't all in agreement about the kind of big and elaborate wedding. Your parents don't have as much money as your intended's parents, and your father is uncomfortable with and a little intimidated by the scale and expense of the plans. Between you and your sweetheart, one of you is wholeheartedly in favor of a big wedding weekend and the other one is not and has pretty well disengaged from much of the planning and the arguments among all the various people.

Our question is, who is placing the primary bets in this situation?

_____

_____

5. You have two candidates to consider for a critical leadership job for your company or organization. Candidate A is kind of a Steady Eddie—he's somewhat quiet, seems to have consistently set pretty ambitious goals, has a good record of doing what he said he would, but is a mediocre public speaker—not terrible but not great. Candidate B is more of a Charismatic Charlie—he's quick to smile and is an absolutely fabulous public speaker. Though he has a mixed record of achievement, he clearly has big ideas and can get people to dream with him.

You can only hire one of the two candidates, and you will lose the other one. Whom do you hire, and why?

___ a.) Candidate A, Steady Eddie

___ b.) Candidate B, Charismatic Charlie

Why: _____

_____

6. You have just made a series of moves with a clear intent in mind—in a business negotiation, in a dating situation, or for your career. But rather than getting closer to your goal, your actions have moved you farther away. Now you see that the predictions you were making about which actions were likely to create which results were way off base—and in retrospect, the error was pretty obvious, not just to you, but to other people with whom you work or socialize.

When you think about a real situation like this that happened to you, how did you feel?

___ a.) Kind of irritated or even angry

___ b.) Kind of chagrined or even ashamed

___ c.) Didn't feel much, I just rolled with it

___ d.) Can't really recall a situation like this

7. Two lifelong friends, nicknamed Fiddle and Faddle when they were just toddlers in the same preschool, have both died at age

eighty-one within a few months of each other—though Fiddle died with a multimillion-dollar fortune now left to charity and Faddle died with far less—and meet again in Heaven. Heaven, they discover, is a pretty cool place with lots of unexpected surprises, one of which is the PI-Meter which provides heavenly measures of earthly performance.

Once they discover this, Fiddle and Faddle ask to see their PI profiles, and immediately the PI-Meter spits out pages and pages with the millions and millions of bets each of them made in the courses of their lives. Yep, makes sense, say Fiddle and Faddle. Then they see that they each have a "betting hit rate," reflecting their "betting averages." Fiddle's score is higher than Faddle's, just as both of them expected given Fiddle's Midas touch.

The last page of the printout shows the final measure, each person's PI level. Fiddle and Faddle take a look, and to Faddle's complete surprise the scores show that Faddle, the one with the lower betting hit rate, had a much higher PI score than Fiddle, the one with the Midas touch. Fiddle begins to laugh, and says, "Ah, just as it should be," and then gives the correct explanation to Faddle.

What does Fiddle now understand and communicate to Faddle?

_____

_____

# THE FINAL ANSWER KEY . . . AND RATIONALES

1. We say, "a.) the quarterback." Here's why. The quarterback's bets—the calls he makes on the field—are a major determinant of whether the team will win or lose, and he and his teammates live with the consequences.

Consultants, on the other hand, *advise* others about how and where to place their bets. If as consultants we tell a steel company to shut down its hot-end operations (where the steel is made and formed into slabs), and then import slabs from lower-cost foreign producers and concentrate on the finishing operations which is where most of the labor input is, that's a big bet—for the steel company. It's a very small bet for the consultants, who can go on to the next project.

*Whether you are the consultant or the client, it's very important to be clear on who is placing the bet.*


2. We assume that most people reading this book would check "b.) keep the old deal," so that's not very interesting to us and probably not to you either. The real questions, and the ones we'll ask you now, are what was the first answer that came into your head and how long did it take you to finally decide on b.).

Betting is a forward activity. On a looking-forward basis, option b.) is a no-brainer as long as you are pretty well convinced that your adversary isn't going to use his or her wealth and achievements to harm you other than for gloating purposes.

Taking less in order to avenge a past grievance is backward thinking. It's also very human and absolutely pervasive in life, politics, careers, and companies. That's one of the reasons we keep talking about "looking into your heart" as an integral part of building Predictive Intelligence—the more you can see where your emotion loops are pulling you backward, the better able you are to choose to live and bet your life forward, rather than to refight past battles.

*All bets start with intent. One of your most important tasks as a bettor is to understand your own intents and whether they are pushing you forward or pulling you back.*

3. Our answer is "a.) Have everyone write down the answer," even if it becomes clear that there are some internal debates and even if not everyone will be correct when the results come back. In fact, when Eileen works with companies, she articulates her own predictions and asks everyone else to do so as well.

The reason for this preference is that when you don't articulate your predictions before you take a bet—in this case, the market research—by the time you see the results you're likely to say, "oh yeah, I knew that," even when you didn't.

Then, because you now think that you already knew what you were going to see when your real predictions were different, you don't change anything or you don't change the correct things. Since you don't see how your understanding of the world has changed, you won't see how you could or should revise your actions as well. You will have learned far less than you could have about how to place better bets in the future.

*Predictions—about what you think you will want in the future and how to achieve these outcomes—are the connective tissue of any bet. Being conscious of the predictions you are making, so you can see which ones were right and which were wrong, is one of the fastest and most effective ways to learn both on a personal level as well as on an organizational level. Every time you learn how to predict better, you up your odds on your next set of bets; and every time you up your odds on your bets, you make your own luck.*

4. This is kind of a trick question. At first glance it may appear that it's the parents and parents-in-law who are placing the bet because the bet is the wedding and they are footing most of the bill for the celebration.

But as this wedding gets planned, the two people getting married are really placing a set of bigger bets about their *marriage*, how they will relate to and care for each other, how they will resolve conflicts, and how they will relate to and deal with each other's families and their demands. If the couple is also contributing to the cost of the wedding, they are also starting their marriage with fewer resources for the early years of their lives together.

*When someone advises you on a bet, whether on how to conduct your life or what company to acquire or anything in between, be sure you know who is going to live with the consequences, especially if the "who" is you.*

5. The choice between the excellent bettor and the great communicator isn't even a contest for us. As long as the job isn't one for which great speech-making is just about the only requirement (a job for a motivational speaker, for example) or we haven't fallen under the voodoo spell of the very charismatic person, we'd always pick "a.) Steady Eddie" (or Edie as the case may be).

People who can create superior "hit" rates on their bets get more of what they want and thereby gain power relative to their goals. To the extent that other people share the same goals, these other people will cede their own decisions and bets to the person who they believe can bet better than they can for that area of their lives, and they will therefore become willing and enthusiastic followers. Peter Lynch, the legendary Fidelity fund manager, has legions of followers. Lynch is a good speaker. His leadership, however, is not based on his speaking ability but rather on his superior "hit" rates. It's what he has done rather than what he says that makes people willing to cede their decisions to him.

In this respect, our thinking runs counter to almost all of the literature on power, leadership, and management. We prefer if our potential leaders are great communicators, because that makes it easier for them to get others to follow them, but we always put a higher weight on the person's ability to see and place the right bets than on his or her charisma.

*To us, the hallmark of great leaders is that they have the capacity to bet well, consistently—they figure out what they need to do to achieve an objective and then they do it. So if you want to be an effective leader, practice your speaking and communications skills, but practice your Predictive Intelligence skills more. And when you select a leader—for yourself, your company, or your country—look more to the person's betting record than to his or her ability to give a great speech.*

**6.** This is one of those questions that has no single right answer, but one very clear wrong one, at least for most people.

The wrong answer is "d.) Can't really recall a situation like this." This is the wrong answer because no one bets right all the time. In baseball, the highest batting average in the major leagues in the past sixty years was Boston Red Sox slugger Ted Williams's .406 in 1941. "Betting averages" are the same in this respect—no one bats a thousand, and no one bets a thousand either.

That's the first aspect of this question. The second aspect is how you *feel* when you realize you've bet wrong, and especially when you realize you missed one of the steps in the Gambler's Dozen. People vary, of course, in their reactions to such situations. And a ping, or the desire to kick oneself in the behind, isn't all bad, because that means that you're recognizing the situation and have the chance to learn from it.

But then you have to move forward and bet forward. Part of learning is taking the lesson, positive or negative, but not taking every loss as a personal defeat nor taking every win as confirmation of your personal and inherent value. You'll continue to make mistakes, and lots of them, but still perhaps not as many and, over time, only a few of the really bad ones.

*As you build your Predictive Intelligence, you won't become a different person. You will become a better version of you, more able to achieve the results that you believe will contribute to the kind of future you want to create. Take pleasure and profit in the game, even when you lose, and keep on learning.*


7. Some people say that success is getting what you want, and happiness is wanting what you get. We say that satisfaction, the last piece of the bet in our diagram, is *knowing what you will want and then placing the bets that will help get you there.* That's what Fiddle finally understands once in Heaven, and that's what Faddle did well on Earth even with a lower "betting hit rate" than Fiddle had achieved.

There are lots of Fiddles in this world, people who, no matter what they have, still want more and therefore always feel impoverished. And they are impoverished, in a way, by virtue of how they've set up their own games.

*Two of the most important, and most often overlooked, pieces of making your luck are steps 1 and 12 of the Gambler's Dozen. Understand what future you want to create and you can choose the bets most likely to get you there. Understand when you've had just enough, and you can use your resources for new endeavors that make more sense to you than fighting old battles or getting more of what you no longer desire. Then, with attention to both the "intent" and "satisfaction" components of your bets, you can make your own luck for creating the future that you desire, by your standards and your goals.*

# The Last Word

You can learn from the past,
but you can't change the past.
Dream forward
and use your Predictive Intelligence to create
the future you want.

# GAMBLER'S DOZEN CHEAT SHEETS

**WE** thought you might like an abridged version of what you've just read—a kind of refresher on key points.

Each cheat sheet for the steps in the Gambler's Dozen has the same format: header plus What, How, and Why:

- The header identifies the step by number and gives its "tag" and its summary question.

- The WHAT gives a short description of what you are trying to do in this step and where it fits in our OOPA! process.

- The HOW provides the top-line bullet points of how to go through this step.

- And the WHY gives you the bottom line of why this step is important for making your own luck.

Feel free to use these cheat sheets in any way that's helpful to you. If you reproduce or distribute them, please include the copyright line at the bottom so other people know where the materials came from. Thanks, and happy betting—

Eileen Shapiro and
Howard Stevenson

# THE SMART GAMBLER'S CREDO

- Every action is a bet

Diagram of a Bet:

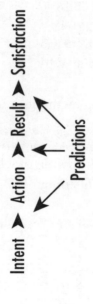

Intent ➤ Action ➤ Result ➤ Satisfaction

Predictions

- You CAN make your own luck

- The key is Predictive Intelligence, the ability to act in the face of uncertainty to bring about desired results

- Improve your Predictive Intelligence and make your own luck by using the Gambler's Dozen

© 2005, Eileen C. Shapiro and Howard H. Stevenson, *Make Your Own Luck*

# BUILD YOUR PREDICTIVE INTELLIGENCE
The OOPA! Process for Making Your Own Luck

## Orient and Organize Skills

1. **The Big Goals:** What future am I trying to create?

2. **Upside/Downside:** Will this game be worth playing, for me?

3. **Jump Bets:** Do I need to make a radical shift now?

4. **Campaign Plans:** Who will I need and how will I get them?

5. **Implicit Strategy:** How much magic will my current bets require?

6. **Plan B:** What's the best I could do if my existing plan gets blocked?

## Predict and Act! Skills

7. **Prediction Maps:** What's the future space I'm betting into?

8. **Wallpaper Jujitsu:** What are my best "left side" bets?

9. **Risk Splits:** How much risk can I shed or shift?

10. **Point of Action:** What's the "it" I'm betting on?

11. **Domino Effects:** Will I be locked into a tight set of follow-on bets?

12. **Game Over:** How will I know when to call it quits?

© 2005, Eileen C. Shapiro and Howard H. Stevenson, *Make Your Own Luck*

# #1: THE BIG GOALS—
## What Future Am I Trying to Create?

**WHAT**

Imagine the future you want to create and envision what your life or company will have to look like to achieve these goals (primarily an OO—Orient and Organize—skill)

**HOW**

*Look Forward, Then Back, Then into Your Emotions*

- Create quick laundry list of your possible objectives
- Pick the "lead dog"—the objective that should get most of the 100 marbles you have to invest
- Work backward from the "lead dog" objective to prune extraneous options from your path
- Check for "emotion loops" that could siphon off some of your 100 marbles

**WHY**

For any bet, you have the equivalent of only 100 marbles to invest. The better you understand, at the beginning of your bet, the future you are trying to create and why, the more wisely you will use the marbles you have—the first step in making your own luck.

© 2005, Eileen C. Shapiro and Howard H. Stevenson, *Make Your Own Luck*

# #2: UPSIDE/DOWNSIDE—
## Will This Game Be Worth Playing, for Me?

**WHAT** Assess whether the game you will have to play—in terms of its upsides, downsides, rules, and rulemasters—will be worthwhile for you according to your standards and values (primarily an OO—Orient and Organize—skill)

**HOW**  *Count Up, Count Down, Then Check the Rules*

- Figure out the upsides that you could achieve (important to do first)
- Look at the downsides and figure out what you *can stand to lose*
- Estimate your likely results if the rules and the rulemakers stay the same
- Assess who could take and keep control of the rules, midgame, and how this could affect your outcomes
- Figure out if you can be the rulemaker and take control of the game

**WHY** To the extent you can, never waste your marbles when your likely downsides outweigh the upsides, or the rules can easily be controlled by people whose interests run counter to yours. Instead, go back to step 1 and invent a different game where you can make your own luck.

© 2005, Eileen C. Shapiro and Howard H. Stevenson, *Make Your Own Luck*

## #3: JUMP BETS—

### Do I Need to Make a Radical Shift Now?

**WHAT**    Be open to unexpected turning points from your planned path— and capitalize on them fast when they look better than staying the course (primarily an OO—Orient and Organize—skill)

*Scan the Horizon and Make the Call*

**HOW**
- Keep a running list of the "neon clues"—events that are clearly unfolding differently than you expected
- Add the "fuzzy clues" to your list—small oddities or a nagging sense that things are out of place
- Make the call, to jump or not to jump, consciously, knowing that you have *incomplete* data
- Then if your call is to jump—jump!

**WHY**    The earlier you can see that an emerging pattern is different than what you expected, the better able you will be to make your own luck by seizing the new high ground and investing your 100 marbles there rather than where you had initially planned.

## #4: CAMPAIGN PLANS—
### Who Will I Need and How Will I Get Them?

**WHAT**

Understand the "people" part of the game you're about to play, and what you'll have to do to get them to participate in the ways and at the times that will be helpful to you—and to them

(primarily an OO—Orient and Organize—skill)

**HOW**

*Think Empathetically and Check the Vapor Trail*

- Work backward from the finish line to sketch out whose help you will need and when
- Use empathy to see which people you can create shared interests with and how to do this
- Sort people into "Core Allies," "The Possibles," and "Null-Setters" to help in this assessment
- Check your past vapor trails and the trail you're about to leave to revise your plans

**WHY**

Empathy is a hidden weapon of a smart gambler. The more you understand the world from the point of view of the people whose help you need, the better able you will be to structure situations in which they will want to invest some of *their* marbles in *your* campaigns.

## #5: IMPLICIT STRATEGY—

How Much Magic Will My Current Bets Require?

WHAT   See and assess your *real* bets (rather than what you tell yourself or others) to determine how much your future success will depend on skill and discipline versus magic and dumb luck (primarily an OO—Orient and Organize—skill)

HOW

*Follow the Currency and Mind the Gaps*

- Determine the "currency"—the kind of marbles (money, time)—used for investing in the bets
- Follow where most of the currency or marbles are going to see the real bets
- Assess how likely your current real bets are to achieve what you want—without a major dose of magic

WHY   Magic thinking is prevalent in corporate bets as well as personal ones. Once you spot this in your own bets, you have the power to change your destiny by either changing your bets to ones with better odds of achieving your goals—or changing your goals to fit your bets.

## #6: PLAN B—
### What's the Best I Could Do if My Current Plan Gets Blocked?

**WHAT**   Think through a Plan B that's solid enough that you could use if you had to—before you find yourself in circumstances that force you to reinvent your bets on the fly (primarily an OO—Orient and Organize—skill)

**HOW**

*Hunt for Elephants and Silver Linings*

- Check for "speedboat wakes"—no Plan B because you've been going too fast to develop one
- Check for "elephants"—no Plan B because no one's been willing to shoot the elephant
- Create a first draft and look for silver linings—new upsides, better ways to mitigate risk, or both
- Decide if any of the Plan B can be incorporated into the base plan; use rest as contingency plan

**WHY**   Time is one of your biggest enemies when events unfold differently than you expected. Make your own luck by having a Plan B in mind, even a rough one, so you're in a position to respond well and in the time available to capture unexpected opportunities or mitigate new risks.

# THE GAMBLER'S DOZEN PREDICTION MAP

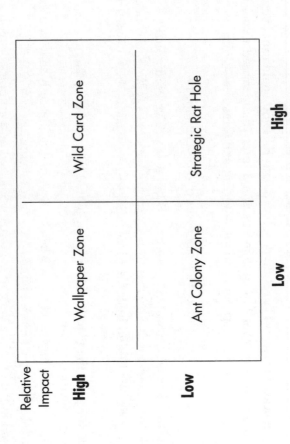

|                    | **Low** Relative Uncertainty | **High**            |
|--------------------|------------------------------|---------------------|
| **High** Relative Impact | Wallpaper Zone         | Wild Card Zone      |
| **Low**            | Ant Colony Zone              | Strategic Rat Hole  |

© 2005, Eileen C. Shapiro and Howard H. Stevenson, *Make Your Own Luck*

# #7: PREDICTION MAPS—
## What's the Future Space I'm Betting Into?

**WHAT**

Forecast the emerging patterns that will have the most significant consequences on your future outcomes in a quick and disciplined way (primarily a PA—Predict and Act—skill)

**HOW**

*Break the Link Between Risk and Return*

- List all the factors that will or could have major future impacts on your objectives—do this quickly
- Sort the factors on the list by how high the future impacts could be on your return
- Do a second sort by uncertainty, high and low, and the risk that you will get a different outcome than planned
- Place the factors on the "Prediction Map" and check and revise

**WHY**

In almost any betting situation, vision and agility will trump brute power. See the emerging patterns first and you have a head start on identifying the sweet spots and required shots for making your own luck.

© 2005, Eileen C. Shapiro and Howard H. Stevenson, *Make Your Own Luck*

## #8: WALLPAPER JUJITSU—
### What are My Best "Left Side" Bets?

**WHAT**

Figure out how to leverage the factors on the left (low-uncertainty) side of the Prediction Map—the Wallpaper and Ant Colony factors (primarily a PA—Predict and Act—skill)

*Focus on the Certain and Do an Empathy Check*

**HOW**

- Imagine the best bets for you to place based on the factors that you have low uncertainty about
- Check and revise these possible bets by thinking empathetically from the other parties' points of view
- Compare the revised "left side" bets with the current bets you're taking or planning to take
- If there's a gap—figure out why and what this means for your current strategy

**WHY**

Bets that leverage Wallpaper factors give the biggest bang with the least risk about future conditions. Smart gamblers invest here and "bet with the house," either to ride a wave that will help them win a goal or to deal with a situation they don't like but understand is coming.

## #9: RISK SPLITS—
### How Much Risk Can I Shed or Shift?

**WHAT** To the extent you have to bet on the right (high-uncertainty) side of the Map—Wild Cards and Strategic Rat Hole factors—find ways to reduce or redistribute the risk (primarily a PA—Predict and Act—skill)

**HOW** *Deconstruct, Recompose (or Bug Out)*

- Identify the most important Wild Card factors
- Construct "Uncertainty Grids" from pairs of Wild Card factors that are reasonably independent
- For each resulting quadrant, ask: if I *knew* this is what would happen, what bets would I make now?
- Look for the bets that work best across the four quadrants
- If all the best bets stink, figure out if this is a game you want to and can bug out from

**WHY** Navigating uncertainty is a fact of life, in business and out. You make your own luck when you understand that risk and return don't have to be perfectly balanced and then find ways to off-load some of the risk and keep the payoff, or keep the risk and up the payoff.

# #10: POINT OF ACTION—
## What's the "It" I'm Betting On?

**WHAT**  Articulate the "it" of your betting plan—the core content of the actions you are going to take, with the intent of creating what outcomes, based on what predictions (primarily a PA—Predict and Act—skill)

**HOW**  *Show the "It" in Three Slides and Check the Links*

- Specify the core content of the product or strategy, and exclude the secondary issues (action)
- Identify the outcomes you are trying to achieve and their future value to you (intent)
- Show your predictions about why you will succeed in the context of your environment (predictions)
- Check the links between actions, intent, and predictions, and your confidence levels

**WHY**  Many companies and many people are precise about the secondary issues and vague about the core "it." This is a losing strategy. If you want to make your own luck, be clear about the core "it" first. If the "it" is solid, fill in the other details. If it isn't, fix the "it" or walk away.

© 2005, Eileen C. Shapiro and Howard H. Stevenson, *Make Your Own Luck*

# #11: DOMINO EFFECTS—
## Will I Be Locked into a Tight Set of Follow-on Bets?

**WHAT**  Understand the degrees of freedom you will have on the follow-on bets you will be signing up for before you topple the first domino (primarily a PA—Predict and Act—skill)

**HOW**  *Check for Two Kinds of Chain Reactions*

- Ask if the bet you're about to take implies a known set of next steps (the "built-in" follow-on bets)
- If not, ask if you can expect major resistance to the outcome you desire (the "bolt-on" follow-on bets)
- If either kind applies, decide if you are prepared to live with these follow-on bets

**WHY**  Some bets come with reasonably predictable follow-on bets. If you aren't prepared to live with these follow-on bets, you'll waste your 100 marbles by taking the first bet. In that case, you'll find that you can make more luck if you rethink your goals and/or your approach.

# #12: GAME OVER—
## How Will I Know When to Call it Quits?

**WHAT**   Figure out how you will know when to call it quits on this game, and either reenter another game with similar rewards or go to a different game that produces a different type of results (primarily a PA—Predict and Act—skill)

*Review the Bet Forwards and Back*

**HOW**
- Look at the expected ratio of upsides to downsides of staying in the current game (predictions)
- Decide if you want the same kinds of upsides or whether you want a different kind (intent)
- See if your past outcomes in this game are pulling you to stay in (satisfaction)
- Decide what is "just enough" for you, so you know when to quit and go to the next game

**WHY**   Every bet—large or small, corporate or personal—puts you into a game. And whatever the game, at some point your participation ends. The question is, do you control the exit because you decide you've had enough and you're ready to go on to the next game, or does someone else?

# Acknowledgments

WE trust that you, the reader, won't be surprised that we followed our own method when we were planning and writing this book. That meant, in the spirit of Chapter 4 on Campaign Plans, that we worked backward from you to reviewers to publishers' sales reps and bookstore buyers to the publisher and finally to what we saw as the starting point, an agent.

And that's where we'll begin our thanks, with our agent, Jim Levine, and his team at Levine/Greenberg Literary Agency Inc. Our research told us that Jim is the best in the business, and so he was the person we sought to represent us. We're glad we did.

This brings us to the second step in our list of whos, our publisher, the Porfolio imprint of the Penguin Group. We liked the Portfolio team, from A to Z—well, really, from C to Z—from the moment we met them: Megan Casey, Stephanie Land, Sarah Mollo-Christiansen, Will Weisser, and Adrian Zackheim.

We're also indebted to several people who read drafts and made corrections and connections through this whole process: Barcy C. Fox of Russell Reynolds Associates, Gary MacDonald of Kingston Technologies, and Lita Nelsen of the Massachusetts Institute of Technology. We also owe a debt of thanks to Carol Franco, and also to Tom Cummings.

And finally, like Fiddle and Faddle, between us we have placed millions and millions of bets over our lives, many successful and many not. To all our friends, colleagues, clients, and family members who have helped us to celebrate when we bet well, and stood with us when we bet poorly and learned a few more lessons, many many thanks.

—Eileen and Howard

# Sources and Notes

Here are the sources we've used and some notes we think may be helpful. For those examples that we use in more than one place in the book, such as General McClellan or the story of the diaper wars, we've tagged our citation and notes to the first reference to the subject in the book.

p. 3, "what we call "Predictive Intelligence . . ."
> *We define the term "Predictive Intelligence" as "the ability to act in the face of uncertainty to bring about desired results." We have used this term for some time. Since developing this concept, we have become aware that other people, including people in the military, also talk about "predictive intelligence" using a variety of definitions. Our usage in this book always refers back to our definition, the ability to act in the face of uncertainty to bring about desired results.*

p. 6, "or as Alan Greenspan, chairman . . ."
> *Alan Greenspan, "Is There a New Economy?," California Management Review*, Vol. 41, No. 1, Fall 1998, pp. 74ff.

p. 8, "Imagine for a moment you are a general . . ."
> *McClellan at Antietam is one of the most studied military battles in history (and especially by generations of Americans growing up south of the Mason-Dixon line). We don't claim to be experts on this battle, only that McClellan's decisions at Antietam provide a dramatic example that every choice is a bet. Two primary sources we used to understand this battle are:*
> *Bruce Catton, The Civil War. Houghton Mifflin, Boston, 1960.
> *Antietam on the Web: http://aotw.org; see specifically "McClellan

Reacts to the 'Lost Order,'" available at http://aotw.org/exhibit.php?exhibit_id=358; this site includes the text of the telegram McClellan sent on September 13, 1862, to President Lincoln. It begins, "I have the whole rebel force in front of me."

p. 10, "Chili Palmer, the low-level . . ."
*Book, originally published in 1990: Elmore Leonard, *Get Shorty*. Bantam Dell, New York, 1990.
*Movie version, *Get Shorty*, 1995. Barry Sonnefeld, director. John Travolta as Chili Palmer.

p. 13, "the level of satisfaction with the actual results achieved . . ."
*We believe that the issue of satisfaction with the bet is one of the most consistently ignored aspects of being a good bettor. Howard has spent a lot of time thinking about and researching this issue, especially in his book* Just Enough.
*Laura Nash and Howard Stevenson, *Just Enough*. John Wiley & Sons, New York, 2004.

p. 14, "Every bet is based on a set of predictions . . ."
*The role of prediction in creating our futures has been a theme in both of our writings, in terms of the power of predictability in creating better futures (Howard) and the effects of poor predictions creating suboptimal results, especially when management techniques are chosen with only slight regard to causes and effects (Eileen).*
*Howard H. Stevenson, *Do Lunch or Be Lunch*. Harvard Business School Press, Boston, 1997.
*Eileen C. Shapiro, *How Corporate Truths Become Competitive Traps*. John Wiley & Sons, New York, 1990.
*Eileen C. Shapiro, *Fad Surfing in the Boardroom*. Perseus Books Group, New York, reprint edition, 1996.

p. 15, "underlying organization . . . is an OOPA! process . . ."
*Students of military history will recognize that our OOPA! process is a variation of USAF Col. John R. Boyd's OODA Loop for military strategy, using the four steps of Observe, Orient, Decide, and Act. We are both fans of Boyd's, and as we worked with his materials, found that we had to modify his approach to match the process we have created. Boyd also comes back in this book in Chapter 7. We used a number of secondary sources on Boyd plus two primary ones, Boyd's 1986 and 1987 military*

*briefings, which describe his ideas and which start with the battles of the Greeks versus the Persians in 490* BC *and the Battle of Leuctra, with the Spartans against the Thebans in 371* BC.

\*John R. Boyd, "Patterns of Conflict," December 1986.

\*John R. Boyd, "A Discourse on Winning and Losing," August 1987.

p. 27, "Dog Haiku"

*We've been asked for the source of this haiku. We wrote it, so the source is Eileen C. Shapiro and Howard H. Stevenson, which means the source line for the haiku is almost as long as the haiku itself.*

p. 30, "what we call the '100 marbles.' . . ."

*When we work with clients, especially smart ones, we often find a curious thing—even PhDs and MDs, when asked how they want to distribute their efforts between three or more goals or activities as expressed in percentages, will often give a set of answers that add up to substantially more than 100 percent. This consistent result has led us to experiment with other ways to make it easier for people to figure out how they want to allocate their resources. The best way we've figured out so far is to pose our questions in very concrete terms, using either 100 items (with each representing 1 percent) or ten items (with each representing 10 percent), which is the genesis of the "100 marbles" metaphor we use in this book.*

p. 30, "Toyota decided to aim at beating . . ."

\*Lee Peart, "Toyota Becomes World's Second-Largest Automaker in 2003," PriceWaterhouseCoopers. Available online at http://www.pwcglobal.com/

p. 33, "was Cytyc Corporation . . ."

\*For more information on this company, go to http://www.cytyc.com

p. 37, "you can cut out many of these potential options . . ."

*In our initial example, we used five steps with each step having four options, which gives $4^5$ or 1,024 options. To continue this example, if by working backward you can cut out two of the options per step, now you have $2^5$ or 32 options toward the same goal. Obviously, there are a number of different reductions you can make in the path (for example, one option at step 1, two options at step 2, three options at step 3, four options at step 4, and five options at step 5, which gives 120 options).*

*The point is, as you work backward, the more extraneous options you can cut from your consideration, the more you can focus your resources on bets that can help you to meet your goals.*

p. 38, "The average American wedding in 2004 cost something on . . ."

*This estimate, $22,360 to be more precise, is from the Condé Nast Bridal Group.* Washingtonian Magazine *puts the cost of the average wedding in 2004 at $28,000. Gerard Monaghan, president of the Association of Bridal Consultants, put it at $24,000, as cited in* The Wall Street Journal *(Mary Kissel, "The Best Woman and Dude of Honor Join Wedding Parties,"* The Wall Street Journal, *August 10, 2004, pp. A1, A6).*

p. 40, "In start-up companies, for example . . ."

*One of the classic articles in this area comes from Manfred E. R. Kets De Vries:*

> *Manfred E. R. Kets De Vries, "The Dark Side of Entrepreneurship," The Harvard Business Review, November–December 1985, pp. 160–67.

p. 45, "Unprecedented and unthinkable."

> *Sarah Ellison, "In Lean Times, Big Companies Make a Grab for Market Share," The Wall Street Journal, September 5, 2003, pp. A1, A10.

p. 47, "Doug Corrigan, one of the . . ."

*A lot has been written about Doug Corrigan. George McEvoy's column when Corrigan died is a nice summary of the spirit of the man. The fiddlersgreen Web site listed below is a good Web source on Corrigan.*

> *George McEvoy, " 'Wrong Way' Was Right on Time," The Palm Beach Post, December 18, 1995, p. 11A.
> *http://www.fiddlersgreen.net/aircraft/wrongway/info/info.htm

p. 53, "what happened to Martha Stewart, convicted . . ."

> *Keith Naughton and Barney Gimble, "Martha's Fall," Newsweek, March 15, 2004, pp. 27ff.
> *Robert Shapiro, "The Basic Rules of White-Collar Defense," The Wall Street Journal, July 10, 2004, p. A10.

p. 61, "as Paul Revere later recounted . . ."
*The Paul Revere story is well known to most American schoolchild-
ren, and the Longfellow poem celebrating the event used to be standard-
issue curriculum for kids in the Northeast. Gladwell, in the best-seller
The Tipping Point, also used Revere as an example.*
  *Malcolm Gladwell, *The Tipping Point*. Little, Brown, Boston,
    2000.
  *"The shot heard round the world," in Hubert H. Bancroft, ed., *The
    Great Republic by the Master Historians,* 1900. This text has
    been excerpted and is available online at http://www.publicbook
    shelf.com/public_html/
  *Department of Military Science at Worcester Polytechnic Institute at
    http://www.wpi.edu/Academics/Depts/MilSci/BTSI/Lexcon/
  *Henry Wadsworth Longfellow, "The Midnight Ride of Paul Re-
    vere," poem first published in 1861 in *The Saturday Evening
    Post,* then included in Wadsworth's *Tales of a Wayside Inn,*
    1863.

p. 64, "to bring forth a new nation, conceived in liberty . . ."
*This phrase comes from Abraham Lincoln's Gettysburg Address.*

p. 72, "Satellite Business Systems (SBS), founded in 1975 as a . . ."
*There's not much of a record left on SBS, but at the time of its exis-
tence, SBS was considered a hot company. Two sources are:*
  *Jonathan McDowell, "Jonathan's Space Report," available online at
    http://host.planet4589.org/space/jsr/back/news.56
  *Tag's Broadcasting Services, "The Satellite Encyclopedia," available
    online at http://www.tbs-satellite.com/tse/online/prog_sbs.html

p. 72, "Ten years later, Iridium, a . . ."
*For a brief summary of Iridium see:*
  *"Iridium (satellite)," entry in "The Free Dictionary," available online
    at http://encyclopedia.thefreedictionary.com/Iridium

p. 74, "Saint Peter Speaks"
*This puzzle is based on a joke we have heard, but we don't know its
origin.*

p. 77, "a caller who keeps the dance moving with a set of patter sayings . . ."
*Square dance "patter sayings" are rhymes or jingles said by callers*

*while the dancers are executing a long sequence such as "Promenade Home." A great site on American square dances and their cousin, quadrilles, is Vic and Debbie Ceder's Square Dance Resource Net. For a list of traditional patter sayings, several of which we used in this chapter, go to this part of the Ceder site:*
　*http://www.ceder.net/choreo/patter_sayings.php4

p. 88, "Miss Mississippi, 1959"
　*This comes from one of Eileen's favorite novels:* Fannie Flagg, *Daisy Fay and the Miracle Man*. Warner Books, New York, 1992.

p. 93, "the diet industry . . ."
　*Diet statistics: U.S. Centers for Disease Control's National Health and Nutrition Examination Surveys, U.S. Department of Agriculture's Economic Research Service, and Marketdata Enterprises, Tampa, FL.

p. 94, "cut out a net 75 to 150 calories a day, . . ."
　*We understand that there are many ways to lose weight, and also that people vary in which methods will suit them best. We also believe that it is highly unlikely that the peoples of North America and Europe in the aggregate have undergone a massive change in their genetic makeup in the past twenty-five years such that they now are more predisposed to be overweight or obese. Instead, our hypothesis is that many of these people are the weights they are because they take in more calories than they expend. The point of this example is the need to understand your own implicit strategy—for your company, your career, or even your diet.*

p. 96, "the case of Mercury Power, in New Zealand . . ."
　*Not surprisingly, this situation was widely followed in New Zealand but hardly covered in the U.S. press at all. For this reason, most of key sources we used for this story come from the NZ media.*
　*Michael Field, "New Zealand Faces Economic Misfortune as Auckland's Heart Loses Power," *Agence France Presse*, February 21, 1998.
　*Denise McNabb and Yvonne Martin, "Cable Failure Raised in 1990," *The Dominion*, February 23, 1998.
　*Denise McNabb and Yvonne Martin, "Blacking Out a City," *The Dominion*, February 23, 1998.

*Simon Jones, "Dying Mercury Boss, 'It's Helped Me Cope with Power Crisis,' " *Sunday Star-Times*, March 1, 1998.
* "What Others Are Saying," *The Evening Post*, March 2, 1998.
* "Report Cites Mercury for Cable Crisis," *The Press*, May 9, 1998.
*Bill Rosenberg and Jane Kelsey, "The Privatisation of New Zealand's Electricity Services," prepared for the International Seminar on the Impact of Privatization of the Electricity Sector at the Global Level, Mexico City, September 20–27, 1999.

p. 98, "what Collins and Porras . . . call a BHAG . . ."
*Jim Collins and Jerry I. Porras, *Built to Last*. HarperCollins, New York, 1994.

p. 101, "Peanut Butter and Jelly"
*This is another old joke whose origin neither of us knows.*

p. 105, "Thomas Hoving, . . . son of . . ."
*The best source on Hoving at the Met is Hoving himself.*
*Thomas Hoving, *Making the Mummies Dance*. Simon & Schuster, New York, 1993.

p. 105, "the Steve Martin classic 'King Tut' "
*http://www.stevemartin.com/world_of_steve/television/kingtut.php

p. 107, "how Beane joined the front office . . ."
*Michael Lewis, *Moneyball*. W. W. Norton, New York, 2003.

p. 119, Teen Haiku
*We wrote this one too.*

p. 121, "say, broadband access to the Internet . . ."
*The problem of overcapacity in industries has been studied extensively, including an excellent summary and analysis in Michael Porter's book,* Competitive Strategy *(Free Press, New York, 1980). In the late 1990s, the telecommunications industry was the poster child for this cycle of growing demand, capacity expansion, and then overexpansion. Two factors that fed this massive and fast capacity expansion were the Telecommunications Act of 1996 and how the Federal Communications Commission (FCC) oversaw and implemented this law. Among the many analyses of the resulting gluts and their consequences are:*

*Jeffrey A. Eisenach, "The Real Telecom Scandal," *The Wall Street Journal*, September 30, 2002.
*Michael A. Hiltzik and James F. Peltz, "Did Telecom Reformers Dial the Wrong Number?," *Chicago Tribune*, July 24, 2002.

p. 122, "Col. John Boyd, USAF, . . ."
*In addition to Boyd's classic briefings cited earlier, two good sources on Boyd in Korea include his obituary in* The New York Times *and the Web site below:*
*Robert McG. Thomas Jr., "Col. John Boyd Is Dead at 70; Advanced Air Combat Tactics," *The New York Times*, March 31, 1997.
*http://www.sci.fi/fta~/JohnBoyd.htm

p. 130, "that 'one if by land and . . .' "
*For those not versed in U.S. (or, to be even more parochial, Boston-area) history, the colonists had arranged for signal lamps to be lit in the belfry of the Old North Church in Boston to indicate which of two routes to Lexington the British were embarking on. The phrase itself comes from the Longfellow poem "The Midnight Ride of Paul Revere" (1861).*

p. 131, "As in the Christmas carol, . . ."
*The Christmas carol is "Santa Claus Is Coming to Town," written by Haven Gillespie and J. Fred Coots in 1934, and includes the line "He's making a list/and checking it twice/going to find out who's naughty or nice."*

p. 133, "the better he controls the strike zone, . . ."
*This is from Lewis,* Moneyball.

p. 139, "in the 1940s, Preston Sturges was . . ."
*Bob Thomas, "Satirist Sturges Remembered on 100th Anniversary of His Birth," *Cape Cod Times*, August 30, 1998, p. D-5.

p. 144, "Desktop computing was just beginning then [1980], . . ."
*If you are curious to see what the old IBM 5150 looked like and its specs—from its Intel 8088 (4.77MHz) and its 16K RAM (expandable to a maximum of 640K)—go to http://oldcomputers.net/ibm5150.html. Also see:*

*Andrew Pollack, "Big I.B.M.'s Little Computer," *The New York Times*, August 13, 1981.
*CBSNews.com, "PC Turns 20." Available online at http://www.cbsnews.com/stories/2001/08/10/tech
*Rachel Konrad, "Special Report: Mixed Record as IBM PC Turns 20," ZDNet UK, August 11, 2001. Available online at http://news.zdnet.co.uk/business
*A great source on the history of computers, from just about the beginning of time to the present, is from Computer Hope:*
*http://www.computerhope.com/history

p. 145, "to IBM's president, John Opel . . ."
*Dick Reiman, "The Personal Computer, Part 9: The Reemergence of IBM." Available online at http://ieee.cincinnati.fuse.net/reiman/01_1999.html

p. 148, "in the early days at the Weather Channel, . . ."
*Frank Batten was the inspiring source behind the Weather Channel; his first-person account is:*
*Frank Batten with Jeffrey L. Cruikshank, *The Weather Channel*. Harvard Business School Press, Boston, 2002.

p. 149, "citizens of Troy saw a gigantic wooden horse . . ."
*No, we didn't go back to the original sources, but we did go to the next best source, Edith Hamilton.*
*Edith Hamilton, *Mythology*. Penguin, New York, 1940.

p. 162, "if you've ever done traditional scenario planning, . . ."
*Three grand-daddy texts on this are:*
*Pierre Wack, "Scenarios: Uncharted Waters Ahead," *Harvard Business Review*, June 1985.
*Peter Schwartz, *The Art of the Long View*. Doubleday Currency, New York, 1991.
*Kees van der Heijden, *Scenarios: The Art of Strategic Conversation*. John Wiley & Sons, New York, 1996.

p. 163, "at the time that IBM introduced the 5150 with Microsoft's DOS . . ."
*Wikipedia, "IBM PC Compatible." Available online at http://en.wikipedia.org/wiki/IBM_PC_compatible

*"HP Timeline—1980s." Available online at http://hp.com/hpinfo abouthp/histnfacts/timeline/hist_80s.html

p. 165, "at twenty-eight pounds, the first 'luggable' . . ."
*If you were born in the 1980s or later and can't imagine what the Compaq Portable looked like, go to http://oldcomputers.net/ compaqi.html. Incidentally, this box had an Intel 8088 processor (4.77MHz), and 128K RAM, expandable to a maximum of 640K.*

p. 165, "Fast forward two decades, and HP had acquired . . ."
*Michael Kanellos, "HP Back on Top of PC Market," CNET News.com, January 14, 2004.
*"Gartner Dataquest Says PC Market Experienced Slight Upturn in 2002, but Industry Still Shows No Strong Rebound." Available online at http://www4.gartner.com/5_about/press_release/pr17Jan2003a.jsp

p. 167, "didn't really look like Microsoft got the Internet . . ."
*Kathy Rebello, "Inside Microsoft: The Untold Story of How the Internet Forced Bill Gates to Reverse Course," *Businessweek*, August 24, 1998. Available online at http://www.businessweek.com/ 1998/35/z3484001.htm

p. 168, "these are the 'skunkworks' projects . . ."
Thomas Peters and Robert Waterman, *In Search of Excellence.* Harper & Row, New York, 1982.

p. 173, A Sad Limerick
*We wrote this one too.*

p. 177, "Consider Iridium, perhaps the poster child for . . ."
*Iridium is a company that we both followed at the time, primarily because we didn't see how the enterprise would survive. There are a number of excellent sources on Iridium; the one we relied on is the Thunderbird case prepared by Professor Andrew Inkpen.*
*Andrew Inkpen, *The Rise and Fall of Iridium.* Thunderbird, the American Graduate School of International Management, 2001.

p. 180, "It is impossible for the drivers to keep . . ."
*Patrick Ryan, "Get Rid of the People, and the System Runs Fine," *The Smithsonian,* September 1977, p. 140.

p. 180, "Coke's 2004 'armpit' commercial spot, . . ."
    *Betsy Mckay and Chad Terhune, "Coke Pulls TV Ad after Some Call
        It the Pits," *The Wall Street Journal*, June 8, 2004.
    *Kenneth N. Gilpin, "Passed-over Coke Executive to Quit," *The New
        York Times*, June 10, 2004.

p. 183, "the 'good deal' test, . . . "
    *Eileen uses the good deal test as part of the "good deal at a profit
    over time" standard she uses to assess business health; see* Fad Surfing in
    the Boardroom.

p. 186, "the opportunity to pay a lot more than the ground-based
mobile . . ."
    *Some of our data on competitive prices in 1998 came from this 1998
    site: http://www.usatourist.com/english/tips/phones.html*

p. 186, "company's assets were purchased for $25 million by . . ."
    *Margo McCall, "Plans for Iridium Back in Orbit," *Wireless Week*,
        November 20, 2000.
    *The current company is called Iridium Satellite LLC. Its Web site is:*
    *http:www.iridium.com.

p. 197, "Cambridge's 1970 rent-control law . . ."
    *For two extreme views on the Cambridge rent-control history, from
    both the left and the right within Cambridge, see:*
        *Patricia Cantor, "How Did It Happen?," *National Housing Institute*,
            1995. Available online at http://www.nhi.org/online/issues/80/
            massrent.html
        *Glenn Koocher, "History of What Was Really behind Rent Control
            in Cambridge," Small Property Owners Association (SPOA).
            Available online at http://www.spoa.com/pages/koocher.html

p. 198, "experiments in Germany and France . . ."
    *Daniel Schwammenthal, "Auf Wiedersehen to the 'Leisure Econ-
        omy,' " *The Wall Street Journal*, August 2, 2004, p. A11.

p. 198, "Kidde to ignore the claims of a small start-up, X-IT . . ."
    *Deborah Elkins, "Record $116M Verdict in 'Copycat' Ladder Case,"
        *Virginia Lawyers Weekly*, 2001.
    *Ilan Mochari, "Climbing Back Up," *Inc.*, March 2002.

p. 209, "the point that AT&T got to in 2004 . . ."

*Shawn Young, "AT&T Board May Pull Plug on Consumers," *The Wall Street Journal*, July 21, 2004, pp. B1, B8.

*CNNmoney, "AT&T 2Q Net Drops 80%; Confirms Consumer Service Exit Plans." Available online at http://money.cnn.com/services/tickerheadlines/for5/200407220734

p. 209, "what John Tu and David Sun did when they . . ."

*The best source on this is Kingston's own Web site, http://www. kingston.com*

# Index

*Page numbers appearing in italics refer to tables and figures*